My Time In His Hands

Christine Wood

Christian Focus Publications

Dedicated to the ladies
who study the Bible with me,
and in loving memory of
Gladys Walton and Peggy Rowbotham.

All the people in this book are real but some names and chronology of events have been changed in order to preserve anonymity.

The quotation from W. Phillip Keller's book *Walking with God* is used by kind permission of Kingsway Publications, Eastbourne.

Published by
Christian Focus Publications Ltd
Geanies House, Fearn, Ross-shire,
IV20 1TW, Scotland, Great Britain.

Cover design by Donna Macleod

Contents

FOREWORD

I have often wondered why it is that we do not all travel along the road of Christian discipleship at the same rate. We grow old at the same rate! A year for a teenager is exactly the same length as it is for someone in their seventies - though of course the feelings may be vastly different. But progress in the spiritual is not as fixed as it is in the natural. Some grow more rapidly in five years than others do in fifty. Why?

I think one answer could be that given by a theologian of great repute who said: 'When we can pause before each one of life's baffling and perplexing situations and seek to draw from them the things God wants us to discover we can rest assured that we are moving along the path to maturity at a speedy pace.'

By this criterion, Christine Wood (though I know she would not agree) shows herself in this book to be ahead of many of us as she demonstrates, albeit unintentionally, her willingness and eagerness to 'pause before each of life's baffling and perplexing situations' and wrest from them the things God wants her to discover.

I have long admired Christine's writing style and ability and in her new book *My Time in His Hands* it is obvious that every word has gone through the crucible of her own experience and emerges finely honed and polished. She does not waste pigment as she paints with words, but shows in the recounting of her experiences the importance of turning each one of life's situations into a stepping-stone to draw still nearer to God.

From the feelings that follow the death of a loved one to the irritation that arises when served by an inefficient shoe salesgirl, Christine underlines the importance of tuning in to what God is saying in all situations. It is a way of living we all need to learn more deeply, myself included, and I am grateful–as I know you will be –for the reminder to turn all difficult situations into prayer and become more sensitive to what God might be saying.

My Time in His Hands reinforces in anecdotal form the thrilling truth that God is involved in what we might consider are the smallest and most insignificant details of our lives. And his timing is always perfect. He is never a moment too soon, and never a moment too late. Looking for him, learning from him, and making 'all things serve' is a spiritual art form that I covet for my own life. Christine has helped me understand this a little more. I think her book will do the same for you too.

Selwyn Hughes
15 November 1993

Chapter One

'This anorak leaks. I'm soaked,' my husband complained.

'What holiday weather! I'll be soaked too if this umbrella capsizes,' I replied, head down against the wind and driving rain.

'What about something to eat in that hotel?' Douglas suggested.

We enjoyed lunch-time snacks in hotels we couldn't afford to stay in, so we turned away from the heaving, frothing sea to seek refuge across the road. We ordered coffee and sandwiches and relaxed in the warm, comfortable lounge.

After visiting the powder-room, I paused to look at the stately grandfather clock in the hotel foyer. The floral design round the roman numerals fascinated me and I studied it in detail. The old clock ticked on, unaffected by my admiration.

Suddenly time seemed to stand still and in those suspended moments an idea formed in my mind. Why not write a children's book centring round a grandfather clock?

Ideas whirred and my mind raced as I listened to the measured ticking of the clock. Instead of a floral design, my grandfather clock would be inscribed above the roman numerals with the words, 'Your time is in my hands,' a turn-around of David's statement in Psalm 31. 'My times are in your hands,' the psalmist had affirmed to God and as I gazed at that stately old clock, his words came alive in a new, fresh way. What a confident affirmation!

'Your time is in *my* hands,' the clock seemed to stress. But it could mark out only the hours that were mine, whereas David asserted something far more significant. I pondered the difference while I watched the minute hand move slowly and steadily round the ornate clock face.

'Penny for your thoughts. You look miles away,' a voice whispered in my ear.

'You made me jump!' I exclaimed, turning to Douglas. 'Actually I was thinking that this clock, any clock, records the hours and minutes that make up our days, but it's God who controls what happens during those hours. You know, like David said.'

'Well, I say the rain's eased so it's time to battle against the sea breezes again,' Douglas smiled.

As we walked along the front we watched black, looming clouds chasing one another and listened to the wind-torn waves casting themselves on the rocks, but still my thoughts on time persisted.

'I wonder when David told God that his time was in his hands,' I said as we sheltered from the wind behind an ice-cream kiosk. 'Perhaps it was after he had been crowned king of Israel. The going would have been good then, when he enjoyed the comforts that wealth can bring. Imagine it, a palace to live in, servants to wait on him and

7

many children to amuse him with their fun and games. It's great that David acknowledged God's goodness.'

'If I remember rightly, it wasn't in those circumstances at all, but we can check,' Douglas replied.

Later that afternoon I turned to the psalms and found that Douglas had been right. Psalm 31 said nothing about easy, gracious living, but focused on adversity, affliction, enemies, grief, weakness, terror and fleeing for refuge. In the midst of all that, David had declared his complete trust in God.

I shut my Bible and watched a fishing boat fighting its storm-tossed way to the quayside. The psalmist's words raised questions in my mind. Had God led and guided me all my life? If so, why had the going sometimes been so hard? Had he really been in control of the disappointing times and during painful, anguish-filled hours? Had David ever wondered too?

While I mulled over these questions a shaft of late afternoon sunlight burst through the clouds, turning the quayside water into liquid gold. The beauty of that old Flemish built quay lured me onto the balcony of our holiday flat to enjoy air enriched by the salt breath of the sea.

Another fishing boat approached and, as I leaned on the balcony to watch, the years slipped away to my childhood at Westcliff-on-Sea. There I had watched many such red-sailed boats move slowly up the Thames estuary. The beauty of those boats sailing towards the setting sun always moved me deeply. My throat would constrict and tears fill my eyes. That is a cherished memory, but not all my childhood memories are as pleasant.

When I was nine years old my father returned from his post in India. I had not seen him for three years, when he had come home on furlough for three months. Although he ignored my brother and me for most of that time, childhood is very resilient. Full of optimism, I imagined that he would treat us differently once we lived together all the time. He would play with Jack and me and take us out. He would also give us special treats such as our friends enjoyed. So much for wishful thinking!

My father arrived on a dull November day but my mother had taken us shopping. He waited outside the block of flats where we lived until we came home. He then kissed my mother but ignored Jack and me, a replay of what I recalled from three years previously. Then my parents had met along the sea front and walked off together. They left me to trail behind, feeling miserable and unwanted. We met Jack from school, but Father ignored him too.

I cannot recall that we talked much about the rejection that we both felt so keenly but I do remember waking one night to the sound of Jack sobbing. I crept to his bedroom and he sat bolt upright at my nearly silent approach. I switched on the light to find him staring at me, his big brown eyes wide with fright.

'What's the matter?' I whispered.

'I thought you were Dad coming to kill me,' he replied.

Although Jack was nearly two years my senior, I sat on the bed and did my best to comfort him.

'Dad's been grumbling to Mum about our school fees and the new shoes I need. He says I can't have any shoes,' Jack went on, with renewed sobs.

I knew exactly how he felt because I, too, suffered the shame of wearing a winter coat let down at the hem and sleeves.

'It's horrid the way you can see where my coat's faded,' I told Jack. 'One of the nuns at school asked me why I wore such old clothes. "Surely your parents can afford a new coat for you," she said. I felt awful but I couldn't tell her that Dad hated me, could I?'

'One night he'll kill us with the carving knife,' Jack predicted and I had a hard time consoling him and quieting my own fears.

'He'd be hanged for killing us,' I said brightly, and that cheered Jack up.

Although in the same predicament, we two reacted quite differently. Jack gradually became withdrawn and inhibited and struggled with a lack of self-confidence until his early death at twenty-one.

With me, the initial deep hurt of rejection gave place to anger. Anger, in turn, gave place to a fierce independence that made me a loner for several years.

But life had its compensations. After my father came home I enjoyed more freedom than I had known before. My parents allowed me to do what I liked during school holidays and I made the most of my freedom.

I loved roaming the seashore searching for shells, or running out on the mudflats. Sometimes I explored nearby woodland, finding endless fascination and delight along its leafy tracks. I loved the primroses and violets that grew under the bushes, and the bluebells that carpeted clearings among the trees. I also learned to look for birds' nests, and to stand very still as I watched the parent birds feed their young.

One showery spring day I discovered an old apple tree growing among some hawthorn bushes and climbed its gnarled trunk to sit among the pink and white blossom. The sun shone briefly on raindrops that, to my enchanted eyes, immediately became diamonds nestling among the delicate blooms.

'It's lovely, Jesus!' I exclaimed, filled with awe of the God who seemed so close, rather than the far off Being I learned about at the convent school.

In a childlike way I felt grateful to the God who delights us with apple blossom in the spring, although as yet I had no sense of a personal commitment to him. On the contrary, my aloneness made me strong and resource-ful, capable of looking after myself and finding my own pleasures.

As I sat among the apple blossom that day I had yet to learn that it is possible to be too independent, too determined (pig-headed, my mother would have called it) and that this can lead to painful consequences.

****

On one of our few sunny afternoons during that Cornish

holiday, Douglas and I relaxed on a clifftop and gazed out to sea. As I gazed my thoughts on time went on expanding.

'You're day-dreaming,' my husband said, with a gentle nudge.

We had sat silently for so long that I had become totally absorbed in my musings, almost forgetting his presence.

'I've been thinking about the children's book I wanted to write when I saw the grandfather clock in that hotel. I've a feeling that my thoughts aren't suitable for such a book after all,' I replied, with a rueful smile.

'Never mind. Write an adult book instead,' Douglas suggested, and this book was born as a result of that suggestion.

****

It is hard to say when I first became aware of time. Punctuality must have instilled some awareness into me when I began school, but my mind flicks back only to the tender holiday romance I enjoyed when eleven years old.

My mother had four unmarried cousins who ran a hotel in Torquay. Whenever we stayed there Auntie Winnie, as I called one of these cousins, always gave us a warm welcome.

'You'll like Gordon, who will soon be here. His parents bring him every August, so we know him well,' Auntie Winnie told me on one visit.

When Gordon, auburn-haired and freckled, arrived we took to each other on sight. We spent many hours together during that magical fortnight exploring country lanes, playing on the beach, or splashing about in unpolluted, crystal clear water. One sunny morning we walked hand-in-hand through the hotel vegetable garden. At the far end we paused beside a huge sunflower to kiss each other, unaware that Auntie Winnie could see us from her office window. I recall looking up at the big sunflower head, which seemed to nod and smile a blessing upon our young love.

'Will you marry me when we're older?' Gordon asked, and I promised that I would.

'We can't get engaged yet, but we will when I've saved up for a ring,' Gordon went on, and my heart took wings.

Our holiday ended the next day so we rose early to make the most of our brief time before parting.

'I'd like you to come to Cockington Forge, but we'll have to hurry,' Gordon said mysteriously, and off we ran.

The furnace already blazed when we panted up to the forge and the blacksmith shod a horse while we watched. When the owner led the horse away, Gordon whispered something to the blacksmith who laughed as he set to work again. Before my fascinated eyes he made the tiniest horseshoe I have ever seen. He brought it to us still hot and charged threepence for it. Gordon wrapped the horseshoe in his handkerchief and off we ran.

'This is for you to keep until I can buy a ring,' Gordon said, back at the hotel.

He pressed the tiny horseshoe into my hand and my fingers closed round its U-shaped warmth.

'You will come here next August, won't you?' Gordon asked and I assured him that I would.

We parted after breakfast but my heart sang all the way home. I did not share my precious secret with my mother though. I feared she would not approve of my 'romance'.

In the following months I pestered my mother to promise that we would go to Auntie Winnie's again for next year's holiday. At last she said we could. She asked no questions, but my whoop of delight must have puzzled her.

'Jack isn't going to Scout camp next summer, so he'll be coming too,' she said, but my brother wasn't the boy who interested me then.

August seemed a lifetime away but I had the tiny horseshoe to treasure until Gordon and I met again. I often took it from its hiding place to look at it, handle it, and remember its warmth when Gordon gave it to me.

At last school holidays drew nearer and my spine tingled at the prospect of once again exploring Devon lanes with my freckle-faced sweetheart. Had he bought me a ring, I wondered. Would my mother allow me to wear it? Should Gordon ask her permission for us to become engaged? I had misgivings about her reaction to that since I was still only twelve.

Apart from my mother's approval, everything seemed set fair for young love to blossom into a second summer's romance. My knees trembled when we arrived at Arlington Hotel but Gordon had not come yet. I hovered round the entrance hall as further guests arrived until my irate mother found me and told me to wash and change for dinner.

The gong sounded, but still no Gordon. Sick with disappointment, I hardly ate a mouthful. Day after miserable day dragged by but on Friday my hopes revived. Surely Gordon would come tomorrow with other new guests.

Once again I hovered round the entrance hall, but still no Gordon. My disappointment during that second week seared even deeper than during the first, and my mother railed at me in exasperation.

'You pestered me to come here, but have been thoroughly grumpy ever since we arrived,' she stormed. 'I've a good mind to take you home.'

I burst into tears and wished she would, but told her nothing of my crushing heartbreak.

On Saturday Auntie Winnie emerged from her office to see us off.

'By the way, Christine, Gordon's coming this afternoon,' she said. 'Shall I give him your love?'

A swipe round the face could not have stunned me more. Turning to my mother, Aunt Winnie smiled indulgently.

'Those two looked so sweet last year. I watched them kissing down by the sunflowers,' she said.

How I hated Aunt Winnie! I felt betrayed, humiliated, and never wanted to see her or Arlington Hotel again.

My tears flowed unchecked on the way home, to my brother's bewilderment.

'Whatever's the matter?' he kept asking.

Because I felt he really cared, I eventually sobbed out my bitter disappointment.

'You brought this on yourself, you know,' my mother said. 'If you had told me how much you wanted to see your holiday friend again, I could have booked the right fortnight with Aunt Winnie.'

We never went to Arlington Hotel again. When war clouds loomed closer my mother's cousins sold it and we went to Falmouth instead.

I have treasured Gordon's little horseshoe for more than fifty years. Among other things, it reminds me of the importance of not only doing the right thing, but doing it at the right time.

And nowhere has that been more true than in my personal walk with God.

Chapter Two

'Keep in time!' the music teacher's shrill voice kept urging, when school re-opened that autumn.

She was talking about music, which some of the class, including myself, murdered by singing out of tune at the tops of our voices.

'Keeping in time is such an important life principle,' Miss Pringle added, pushing back a strand of greying hair from her lined forehead.

She did not explain with whom or what one should keep in time (other than music), but her statement felt like salt in a wound after my 'timing tragedy' in Torquay. To this day her words have retained a significant place in my memory.

That same term Wendy, one of my school friends, invited me to a Girl Crusader Class. I had no idea what Crusaders stood for but went because I liked my cheerful, dimple-cheeked friend.

This homely Bible Class, as it turned out to be, took place in the Assembly Rooms opposite our school. I felt drawn to Miss Grove, the kindly, gentle teacher, from the start. Sunday by Sunday she held me spellbound as she brought stories from the Gospels alive to me in a new, fresh way.

In my imagination I saw Jesus being baptized in Jordan, watched him heal the sick, the lame, the blind. As

Miss Grove talked, I also watched Jesus walk by Lake Galilee, and heard him say to Peter and Andrew, 'Follow me'. I caught awed glimpses of him suffering anguish in the Garden of Gethsemane, and blinked back the tears when brutal hands nailed him to a cross.

God's love glowed through Miss Grove and I felt its warmth. She told us girls that God, our Heavenly Father, loved us more deeply than the best human father could ever do. Her words burst onto my consciousness like wonderful shafts of light. I found this marvellous news almost too much to take in. My human father had rejected me at birth and that rejection remained total. But I had a Heavenly Father who loved me!

One never-to-be-forgotten Sunday Miss Grove read to us those familiar words from John's Gospel: 'For God so loved the world, that he gave his only begotten Son, that whosoever believeth in him should not perish, but have everlasting life.'

'Yes, our Heavenly Father loves us so much that he sent Jesus into the world to die for us. He bore the punishment for all the wrong things that we have done. Now salvation is his free gift,' Miss Grove explained.

I lingered behind that Sunday, and as I pulled on my coat Miss Grove put her arm round my shoulders.

'God loves you, Christine. His gift of salvation is for you. Will you accept it?' she asked, and I can still recall the love in her eyes as she spoke.

I could only nod, too overcome for words. But the seed of faith that Miss Grove had planted in my heart took root that day. Joy overwhelmed me as my heart opened to receive my Heavenly Father's astonishing gift.

Another Sunday it thrilled me to learn that, now that I was his child, God had a plan for my life which he would reveal step by step. I understood little about walking by faith, but a year later severe illness tested such girlhood faith as I had.

At first my mother thought I had what would today be called a tummy bug, but the distressing, debilitating symptoms continued day and night. Our elderly doctor talked vaguely about water being low in the reservoirs that year, also about the harmful effects of too much exposure to ultra-violet rays.

'Be sure to wear a hat when you go out, dear,' he said.

'But I can't go out,' I protested.

I had been confined to bed for two weeks and, after stroking his chin, the doctor advised me to stay there. He prescribed a kaolin compound and a monotonous diet of beef broth, white bread and milk puddings. All to no effect. The painful symptoms continued and I daily felt more isolated.

My brother never came to see me as my mother feared he would 'catch' whatever I suffered from. Mother brought me up three dull meals a day, but would not stop to talk or sit with me. I often begged her to read to me but she refused. How to stand alone in suffering, with few words of sympathy, proved a hard but valuable lesson to learn in my youth.

The doctor paid weekly visits and my school friend

Margaret also came on Saturday afternoons. Margaret had large grey eyes fringed with long, dark lashes. She also had two thick plaits. I envied her, since my eyes are brown and my mother insisted that I kept my straight, brown hair cut short. But envy did not spoil our friendship and I longed for Margaret's visits. At my invitation, she had become a Crusader so she told me about Crusader happenings as well as the latest school gossip.

August slipped into September and our garden trees put on their autumn dress of yellow, bronze and golden leaves. I loved slipping out of bed to look at the garden. It was my only visual link with the outside world. October came and went and the leaves fell from the trees. This saddened me but, bedridden as I was, I learned to 'live positively' by keeping myself busy.

I had changed schools shortly before this illness struck and should have been learning shorthand and typing amongst other business subjects. Margaret brought me a shorthand manual and exercise book from school and I taught myself shorthand. Her mother also asked me to embroider a tablecloth that she had kept unworked in a drawer. She supplied plenty of silks so I worked eagerly on this project.

One morning while I sat in bed embroidering, my father flung open the bedroom door and raged at me for being ill for so long. I had not seen him for weeks and, since he never normally spoke to me, this verbal attack shocked and distressed me deeply.

'You're nothing but a nuisance and expense,' he ranted on. 'Who do you think is having to pay the doctor's bills?

And how dare you keep the rest of the house awake by constantly pulling the lavatory chain at night?'

I listened, speechless with guilt and shame. When my father at last slammed the door shut, all joy went from my sewing. I pushed it to one side and sobbed into the pillows.

But my Heavenly Father comforted me in this storm. I heard no audible voice, yet deep within I knew that he was with me, that he loved me, and I calmed down. I also recalled that I had £35 in a Post Office Savings Account. Maybe I would soon be well enough to draw some of it out to pay my own medical bills. That possibility filled me with hope. (The National Health Scheme did not exist then.)

Christmas drew nearer and I shared with Margaret my inability to buy any Christmas presents that year.

'Shall I buy some for you?' Margaret offered.

'Mum hasn't given me any pocket money since I've been ill so I can't even buy cards,' I lamented.

'Actually I think you'll be dead by Christmas, so don't worry,' Margaret said, a cheerful twinkle in her grey eyes.

I, too, smiled with relief. I had no fear of death and knew that Jesus would not tell me off for being ill. Instead he would welcome me into heaven.

After Margaret left I lay very still for a long time and tried to die. While lying there I did a lot of serious thinking for a thirteen year old. Slowly and quietly the inner conviction came to me that, as Miss Grove had said, God had a purpose for my life. Whether short or long, he would be with me and would love me to the end of my life.

But my journey in time proved not to be as short-lived

21

as Margaret had predicted. Christmas saw me slowly regaining health and strength, the distressing symptoms having ceased as suddenly as they began. I well remember my first short walk with Margaret on a cold winter's day. She had just acquired some white mice, two of which she brought round to show me. I put one in each coat pocket, where my gloveless hands gently enfolded their warm, soft little bodies.

In the New Year I forgot the isolation of my bedroom and returned to school. It tired me at first but I was pleased to find I had kept abreast of the other girls in learning Pitman's shorthand.

I also returned to Crusaders and soon became a senior. This meant I had the pleasure of being taught by the class leader, Mrs Green. During the next three years she imparted many spiritual truths which I pondered in my heart.

On my seventeenth birthday this motherly lady gave me a poem by A S Wilson called *Indwelt:*

> Not merely in the words you say,
> Not only in your deeds confessed,
> But in the most unconscious way
>   Is Christ expressed.
> Is it a beatific smile,
> A holy light upon your brow;
> Oh no, I felt His Presence while
>   You laughed just now....

'It's my prayer that this poem will be true of you, dear,' Mrs Green smiled, handing me the card.

22

Although the words moved me, I failed to see myself reflected in them. But I certainly saw Mrs Green:

> For me 'twas not the truth you taught
> To you so clear, to me still dim
> But when you came to me you brought
>   A sense of Him.
> And from your eyes He beckons me,
> And from your heart His love is shed,
> Till I lose sight of you and see
>   The Christ instead.

In his book *Walking With God*, W Phillip Keller says: 'Almost all of us have had men or women cross our paths who were obviously deeply and significantly walking with God ... they made an enormous impact upon us ... Just knowing them induced within our spirits an intense, inner desire to know and walk with God in the same way.' Those words describe exactly how I felt about my Crusader Leader.

One evening Mrs Green invited her senior girls to a 'fireside chat' at her home. I loved those cosy times when we spoke freely of our hopes and dreams and in what ways we would like to serve God. I particularly recall the awed respect I felt for slim, fair-haired Rachel who wanted to be a missionary. I could not imagine anyone so smart and well-groomed making a success of things in the African bush or some malaria-infested area of the Congo, as it was then called. I had no idea how I wanted to serve God but one thing I knew for sure. I had forsaken all ideas I once had of being a missionary.

At the end of the evening Mrs Green turned to Genesis in her Bible and spoke to us about Joseph, whose jealous brothers sold him into slavery in Egypt. I hung on every word as she brought this Old Testament hero alive to us in a fresh and relevant way. I identified with him in his family problems and sympathized with him when unjustly accused of molesting his master's wife and then being thrown into prison.

Mrs Green went on to say that, while still in prison, the jailer ordered Joseph to look after two more prestigious prisoners, Pharaoh's butler and baker. One morning Joseph asked these two why they were so dejected.

He little knew the importance of that question. Joseph asked because he cared, yet his own future destiny hung on that question, its answer, and subsequent events. And not only Joseph's destiny, but that of Egypt and of his own family was also affected.

'It's the timing of this incident that is so precise,' Mrs Green continued. 'Three days after Joseph's kindly question those two officials left the prison. Had Joseph not shown that he cared when he did, he would have missed that life-changing opportunity. Because he asked, his question led to his own liberation and emancipation to Prime Minister of Egypt. He also became the nation's provider in a severe famine.'

As Mrs Green talked I gained glimmers of understanding of God's perfect timing in the lives of those who love him, and the importance of being sensitive to his leading.

The truths that Mrs Green shared that evening, and the

loving, homely way that she did it, so moved me that I closed my eyes to pray one of the shortest but sincerest prayers of my life: 'O Lord, make me like Mrs Green. Please use me to share Bible truths with others too.'

In my earnestness, tears seeped through my closed lids, yet I had no idea how profoundly that prayer, or rather God's answer to it, would affect my pathway through life, nor what hard training it would involve.

As I cycled home that evening I had a glowing, self-confident vision of holding eager listeners spellbound as I unfolded Scripture to them. Shortly afterwards I went to a Girl Crusader's camp. One afternoon I skipped camp activities to read my Bible alone in the woods. This, I decided, would be the day of God's great revelation when he would show me many wonderful truths in his Word which I, in turn, would pass on to others. I had yet to learn that God does not go in for crash courses.

Dappled sunlight danced on the pages of my Bible as I read and re-read Paul's two letters to Timothy. I gained nothing specific from them, nor could I understand much of what I read.

The afternoon shadows lengthened as tears of disappointment wetted the pages. God had not heard my earnest prayer at Mrs Green's house. Or, if he had, he had chosen not to answer. Disillusioned, I snapped my Bible shut and it remained a closed book for many days.

I was not exactly angry with God but frustration ran high because he had not taught me all I wanted to know. I was so set on 'instant illumination' that I failed to realise that God is much more patient and thorough. He teaches 'precept upon precept; line upon line ... here a little, and there a little' - and I needed to keep in time with him, instead of trying to push on ahead. Impatience, my besetting weakness, prevented me from doing this.

That summer Mrs Green began a Friday evening Bible Study for her senior girls. She expected me to come and I can still see her pained expression when I declined. She could not know it, but I still struggled with bitter feelings because God had 'let me down'.

During that afternoon in the woods I had read and re-read Paul's counsel to Timothy: 'Meditate upon these things; give thyself wholly to them', but the message did not sink in.

It was the same with Mrs Green herself. Much as I admired her Christian maturity, I had a mental block regarding the disciplined, Spirit-controlled living that produced it. I knew little of the crosses and sorrows that had mellowed and sweetened her, giving her so much love for us girls.

When Mrs Green invited me to her Bible studies, she told me that I would need to study and meditate upon set Bible chapters before each meeting, which was another reason why I refused to attend. It sounded too much like hard work.

Yet, paradoxically, I still longed to understand the Scriptures so, when what appeared to be an easier, 'instant option', presented itself, I grabbed at it.

Chapter Three

My downfall began during the Second World War. I worked in London, where air raid sirens had sounded several times on that particular day. I left the office feeling strained and heavy-hearted, but it wasn't the war that distressed me. My parents had had one of their many rows. They had not spoken to each other for a whole week since and it had got me down.

I was accustomed to my father not speaking to me but somehow I could not take it when he and my mother weren't on speaking terms either. It had not been so bad when my brother bore such silences with me, but now Jack had joined the army so I endured my parents' private war alone.

On that depressing Friday I alighted from the train at the station before mine to walk the long road home. I preferred the risk of being out in an air raid rather than go straight home to the frigid atmosphere. Tears coursed down my cheeks as I trudged along the almost deserted road and I failed to notice a cyclist until he braked and spoke to me. Even in the fading evening light he had spotted my Crusader badge.

'As you can see, I belong to the Scripture Union,' the cyclist said, patting the small green badge on his lapel. 'I take it you're a Christian too.'

I managed a watery smile and nodded.

'My name's Alf,' the friendly cyclist beamed.

He appeared not to notice my embarrassment as I tried to speak normally. After a long kerbside chat, Alf invited me to a Bible Study at his friend Clive's house.

'He lives in the next road to you, so you won't have far to walk,' he enthused.

At first I felt reticent but Alf persisted, and offered to call for me. I didn't want that. None of my friends called at our house, but I did agree to come to a Bible Study.

Clive's confident bearing and commanding personality made an immediate impact, even if I flinched at the piercing gaze of his light blue eyes. At his house I also met three other young men, who, like myself, worked in a 'reserved occupation' exempting them from military service. Clive's wife Lillian and her friend Pearl, whose husband had just been called up, smiled a welcome that quickly put me at ease.

That first Bible Study held me enthralled and Clive's knowledge of the Scriptures astounded me. He lacked Mrs Green's homely touch but I drank in every word and longed to return for more.

'I hope you'll come again,' Lillian invited over a weak, wartime cup of tea and I assured her that I would.

'Why do you wear that Crusader badge?' Clive asked a few weeks later.

'To show I'm a Christian,' I replied.

'It's a poor sort of Christian who needs a badge to show it,' he said, a touch of asperity in his voice.

His words and tone stunned me. Lillian smiled reassurance but it failed to erase my self-doubt. What sort of a Christian was I? Why so slow to grow in faith and understanding? I branded myself a failure and walked home in despair. Clive's approval of me really mattered, although we were but new friends. Couldn't he see my eagerness to learn? Didn't that count for anything?

Deep feelings of defeat robbed me of sleep. I tossed about, convicted of my poor Christian witness, unaware of my fatal mistake in valuing a friend's opinion of me more than God's. Also, this morbid self-analysis so fixed my gaze on my own spiritual state that self, instead of Christ, filled my view.

'Which church do you attend?' Clive asked on a subsequent visit.

'St. Matthias,' I told him, 'but I'm not all that happy there. The vicar doesn't preach from the Bible much. His sermons are mostly on social or political issues.'

'What else can you expect from the world's system of religion?' Clive asked, his piercing blue eyes cold with disdain.

No one had spoken to me like this before. It sounded a strange, new slant on church-going but, since the services bored me anyway, his criticism provided a good excuse for not going.

'That's right. Keep clear of man-made religious tradition with its dead ritual and ceremony,' Clive advised, rewarding my decision with a smile.

In my brainwashed state I never once paused to

consider where this isolating choice would lead.

Although I revelled in much of Clive's teaching, and respected his learning, questions still troubled my mind. How, for instance, could it be wrong to wear a Crusader badge when Crusaders meant so much to me? I had accepted Christ as my Saviour there and regarded Mrs Green as a fine Christian woman. Was she, after all, in error?

I lapsed into silent confusion until Clive asked me outright what was wrong.

'You disapprove of Crusaders, yet I owe a lot to Mrs Green, our leader,' I replied. 'She's a marvellous Bible teacher.'

'Doesn't she know the Bible says: "I suffer not a woman to teach"?' Clive asked, his voice grave.

This man, who I both admired and feared, spoke with such authority that it did not occur to me that he might be wrong, or that this prohibition of Paul's applied only to certain public occasions.

'Is that all?' Clive persisted, but more gently.

'No, I didn't like what you said about "badge Christianity" either,' I blurted out, fingering my Crusader badge. 'I wouldn't even be here if it wasn't for this badge. Alf only spoke to me because he saw it.'

Clive smiled explaining that God bears with us in our weaknesses but expects us to go on from there.

'God wants us to equip ourselves with his armour as outlined in Ephesians Six, not with badges,' he asserted, his face stern again. 'It's time you grew up spiritually and forgot about childish badge Christianity, fireside chats and girls' camps.'

I listened in uneasy silence, mulled over what Clive told me and eventually accepted the challenge that it would cost me something to be a more mature Christian.

After much heart-searching, I unpinned my badge and left Crusaders. Mrs Green bade me a loving but sorrowful farewell. She had hoped that I would help her start a new junior class after the war and did not hide her disappointment.

'Do nothing in haste. Be very sure of where you are going,' she counselled, but her wisdom fell on deaf ears.

Shortly after this painful parting, I also gave up my non-Christian boyfriend, Peter.

'As a Christian you shouldn't be unequally yoked with a non-believer,' Clive had told me, quoting a verse from Second Corinthians, chapter six.

I regretted mentioning Peter to him, yet, after reading the relevant verse for myself, decided he must be right. The next time Peter came home on army leave I told him that our friendship must end. With so little love in my life, it hurt me deeply to kiss him a tearful farewell.

With these 'victories over the flesh', as Clive called them, to my credit I expected some praise from him. Instead he told me in an oddly detached manner that he had taken me as far as he could spiritually.

'I'm ending the Bible Studies because it's time you sought deeper fellowship in the company of other mature Christians,' he said.

I stared, flabbergasted. Then it dawned on me that he must have said the same thing to the three young men who worked at his factory. At this point a red light presumably shone for them, since none of them came to that last Bible Study and I never saw them again. Only Pearl remained, now a war widow and mother of a baby boy.

Jack, my brother and dear companion in many childhood stresses, had also laid down his arms in the Middle East and lay buried in a military cemetery in Haifa. Mutual sorrow drew Pearl and I close together.

After little Daniel's birth, Pearl's landlady turned her out of her bed-sitter and Clive and Lillian took her in until the end of the war. Had it not been for my close friendship with Pearl, I may well have severed all connection with Clive, since I felt so let down when he ended the Bible Studies. Instead, Pearl and I accepted his invitation to attend the meetings to which he had been linked for many years. And that was my introduction to the Exclusive Taylorite Brethren, who prided themselves on keeping well separated from the rest of 'the world'.

First impressions are hazy but I recall thinking how dull the 'sisters' looked in their drab coats and the quaint old hats pulled well down over their foreheads. No one dressed smartly during or just after the war, but these sisters looked extra dowdy and other worldly.

The 'brothers', also sombrely dressed in black or dark grey, were the only ones permitted to speak in the meetings. Leading brothers sat in the front rows and, since the Exclusives disapproved of Sunday Schools, the

32

married women sat behind with their families beside them. The children looked well-scrubbed and smelt of carbolic soap, yet even in those early days I recall pitying them as they sat, bored and silent, on hard wooden seats.

But the brothers, especially the leading ones, certainly appeared to know their Bibles. And so I remained and adjusted to the unusual set-up as I drank in Exclusive teaching.

I accepted many taboos such as Thou Shalt Not cut thy hair, wear make-up or high-heeled shoes, and much more, since it seemed worth any sacrifice to gain the Truth.

In my ignorance I failed to discern that the Brethren tore many Bible verses from their context, or that they stretched them to a point that bore little relation to the original meaning in order to fit in with the doctrines of the sect's leader, James Taylor.

It both saddens and amazes me now that I spent so long among the Exclusives – wasted years that caused me many heart-searchings and sleepless nights. As time went by it shocked me to discover, through the revelations of special Care Meetings, that the lifestyle of some of the weaker brethren failed to match up to the high moral standards advocated in the meetings.

Disillusionment proved slow and painful, yet a strange reluctance prevented me from leaving this legal, narrow sect. I can only say that continual brainwashing must have paralysed me into believing I would be guilty of a terrible sin if I turned my back on 'the truth as found in the assembly'. Coupled with this fear, pride prevented me from admitting, even to myself, that I had made a serious mistake in joining this sect in the first place.

Weighed against nagging doubts stood the fact that I had made several friends amongst the Exclusives. The more senior brothers regarded some of them as 'weak in the faith' for various reasons, but they accepted me as one of themselves and I needed to be accepted after so much parental rejection. It gave me a sense of identity.

I particularly remember Gaius, who cycled to and from the meetings with me. He often hinted that he would like me for his steady girlfriend. I enjoyed his light-hearted chatter, yet he was not the sort of person with whom I could share my problems, since he avoided serious discussion.

'You know, you'd be much more fun if you weren't so fervent about things,' Gaius once reproved, when I tried to confide in him.

'Your attitude towards the Exclusive teaching is so flippant that I can't understand why you stay with them,' I countered.

Gaius explained that he had a 'weak' brother who had left the assembly. His father had promptly disinherited him and the rest of the family had also cast him off.

'Dad's quite wealthy, so I don't see why I shouldn't hang on until I get my whack,' Gaius told me frankly.

'So it's money and family ties that keep you here, not real faith,' I replied, sickened by his admission.

'I guess I'm not the only one,' he shrugged.

Many years later, after the publication of my autobiography *Exclusive By-Path* , a Mrs Smith wrote to me via the publishers saying how much the book had meant to Titus, her husband, who had been cast off from family and friends upon leaving the Exclusive Brethren.

An inner prompting urged me to tell this lady straight away how pleased I was that the book had helped. Mrs Smith then begged me to visit Titus who, she said, was very unwell. They lived within reasonable travelling distance, so I called on the Smiths and listened to a long, sad tale of family neglect and ostracism. After I had stepped over rolled up carpets and squeezed past large boxes in the hall, Mrs Smith asked me not to stay long as visitors distressed her husband.

'It's just that he so much wants to meet you after reading your book,' she explained.

Two hours later found me still trying to get away from a nervous wreck of a man who could not stop talking. His wife watched in amazement as the frustration, hurt and heartache of years poured from his lips. Once opened, the floodgates refused to shut.

'My brother Gaius died in his forties. I hadn't seen him for years and the Brethren banned me from attending his funeral,' Mr Smith told me, tears streaming down his thin, sorrowful face.

Gaius! Everything slotted into place. This frail little man was the black sheep of the Smith family I had known so long ago. When I at last left, Mrs Smith kissed me at the door.

'I can't thank you enough for being so understanding,'

she said. 'You've done Titus a power of good. What a load he's got off his chest!'

I had done little but listen, yet God's perfect timing over this incident filled me with wonder. I was glad I obeyed that inner prompting to write straight away. Could it be that I was learning to 'keep in step with the Spirit', as the apostle Paul advised?

The Smiths moved two days later. I never heard from them again, but like to think I reassured Titus that he had a Heavenly Father who loved him and would never cast him off.

****

Other Exclusive friends included the Franklins with their large, lively brood of children. The Brethren were not supposed to 'observe times or seasons' but each Christmas the Franklins weakened and had a turkey, Christmas pudding and Christmas tree.

My father loathed Christmas. Since we didn't speak to each other I never discovered why, but the festive season would have been dreary indeed had not the Franklins and other Exclusive families shared their 'forbidden' Christmases with me over the years.

I also recall Miss Rail with special affection. She always looked prim and correct in her plain grey dresses but secretly she read novels – wickedly daring and worldly for an Exclusive sister.

This elderly lady often invited me to tea. At first I

went with some trepidation but soon discovered that her grey dresses hid a heart of gold. I still remember the mischievous twinkle in her eyes when she handed me an innocent-looking brown paper parcel after the 'Breaking of Bread' one Easter Sunday. When I got home I unwrapped a huge chocolate Easter egg. Had the Exclusives known that she 'observed seasons' in this way she would have been reprimanded for such weakness, but to me she was most warm-hearted and lovable.

If anyone stepped too openly out of line, the Exclusives held a Care Meeting to look into the default. This caused a great deal of distress and unrest beyond the boundaries of one's own local assembly, since the Brethren intermarried widely.

Although without such family ties, I suppressed many niggling doubts about the more extreme Exclusive teaching in an effort to be loyal to the sect. Once again I made the fatal mistake of trying to please man rather than God, and so avoided facing up to my misgivings.

The few close friends to whom I dared to mention these doubts appeared apathetic or confused regarding their own beliefs. Others appeared more interested in breaking as many rules as possible without being found out. One friend told me she had been to the cinema with a soldier home on leave, and afterwards had a drink in a pub (all strictly forbidden), while another confided that he and his sister had braved the air raids to see *Me and My Girl* at a London theatre. Others, less daring, used face powder sparingly or painted their nails with transparent varnish (which they covered with gloves during meetings).

In 1954 some Exclusives risked condemnation by going to Harringay to hear the 'heretic' Billy Graham preach. My less adventurous friends settled for a game of pitch and putt on an out-of-the-way miniature golf course.

Despite the forbidden activities that they occasionally indulged in, these friends still remained trapped by their family roots, which spread far and wide amongst the assemblies. In some ways they endured a worse plight than I did since they were victims from birth of a narrow religious system which specialized in Thou Shalt Nots and separation from 'the big, wicked world'.

Not all the Brethren I knew well secretly kicked over the traces. The majority took 'separation from the world' seriously and believed they had a monopoly of truth. By remaining 'outside the camp' (one of their favourite quotes from Hebrews) they supposed that God smiled his approval upon them. I envied these Brethren, and regarded them as the fortunate ones. They had no desire to break the rules, nor did doubts plague them about the rightness of their isolated position.

I once asked a pious young brother what he thought of Christ's command to go into all the world and preach the Gospel.

'How can we do that when we keep apart and don't speak to anyone?' I wanted to know.

'Ah, but our silence condemns,' he replied smugly.

'Condemns who?' I asked, but my question fell on deaf ears.

****

It had been all too easy to join the Exclusive Brethren, but how to extricate myself presented problems. Although I failed to understand what had happened, in fact I had allowed first Clive, and then the Exclusives, to displace God in my life. I lost my commitment to him by becoming a conformist. In so doing I also opted out of the responsibility of making my own decisions, thereby allowing myself to become more and more brainwashed.

Sadly, I all but forgot that I had a Heavenly Father, but how grateful I am that he did not forget me, or that earnest prayer I prayed when seventeen years old.

Chapter Four

Over and above the growing doubts surrounding my association with the Exclusive Brethren, the war took a heavy toll on my emotional, mental and physical reserves. For five wearying years I travelled to London to work, facing up to air raids and never knowing how or when I would get home. Some days I had to ride on a series of buses, with long, dark waits in between, when the railway received a direct hit.

In my debilitated state I did not stop to evaluate what I wanted to gain from life and had no goals other than hoping to become a personal secretary. My attitudes had become largely negative, lacking creative vision, and my relationship with God suffered in that prayer became a virtual non-event and I lost my love for his Word.

After a series of promotions I achieved my ambition and became a personal secretary in the firm for which I had worked since I was seventeen. Pay and prospects looked good but my boss proved an autocratic tyrant for whom I found it hard to work. Exacting and difficult to please, he often made unreasonable demands.

I accepted the challenge, determined to make a go of the job that other young women senior to myself had turned down. Although I coped, it took a further toll on nervous energy and the sheer slog of the work load often exhausted me.

The strain of my home-life remained unchanged. Although the war ended in 1945, my parents' private war dragged on with no sign of a peace treaty and I was often the butt in between their various battles. In some ways the Exclusive meetings on Sundays made a welcome escape, although they were hardly the ideal solution since this association had brought its own tensions.

My health deteriorated under so much stress. It would not have been called this then, but I suffered from what the Americans call burnout. It is a good word as it exactly describes the complete drain of all one's resources.

Although it is a comparatively new word, the symptoms of burnout have been around a long time, even back to Old Testament days. Great achievers like Moses and Elijah suffered from it. David also had his share and became overwhelmed with the desire to 'get away from it all'. In his despair he cried out: 'My heart is in anguish within me; the terrors of death assail me. Fear and trembling have beset me; horror has overwhelmed me ... oh, that I had the wings of a dove! I would fly away and be at rest ...'.

As a youth David had killed a lion and a bear with his own hands. He also killed the giant Goliath with a sling and just one smooth stone. Later David became the greatest of Israel's military deliverers. When he died the territory Israel controlled extended from Egypt's border to the River Euphrates, comprising both Jordan banks and the lands on both sides of the Dead Sea.

Israel proudly proclaimed: 'Saul has slain his thousands, and David his tens of thousands'. Yet when burnout struck, David lost his courage and, like Moses and others before him, he wanted to run away from his problems. It is only conjecture, but maybe at this point he even forgot his previous confident assertion to God: 'My times are in thy hands'.

I empathized with David in my burnout and found comfort in turning to my neglected Bible to read some of his Psalms - heartcries that echoed many of my own, putting them into words more graphically than I could have done. Such self-confidence as I possessed reached an all-time low and I feared that my job would prove too much for me. I felt an utter failure, without knowing that this is yet another symptom of burnout.

In all the pressure the illness from which I suffered when thirteen years old returned. The bout proved less severe and, with the help of medication not available in my childhood, I worked with only occasional sick-leave. After X-rays and various tests, a specialist diagnosed nervous colitis and, because of its persistent nature, I became a regular outpatient at a London hospital.

'I've a feeling you haven't told me what's really bothering you,' the kindly specialist said on my fourth visit. 'That's why you aren't responding to treatment.'

At this invitation I poured out all the frustration and misery of my home-life, the account well-watered with tears.

'Ah, now we have something positive to work on,' the specialist said. 'We can see, can't we, that we must remove the cause of the trouble.'

He suggested that I leave home but that proved easier said than done. I had saved hard during the war and could afford to furnish a flat, but where could I find one? The housing situation remained critical for many years after the war, as many returning servicemen discovered to their cost.

But I refused to give up hope and searched for a small flat. In my distress I even drew nearer to God again and prayed for a home of my own, no matter how humble.

I often lay awake mentally furnishing my dream home with 'utility', post-war furniture. I would have a beige carpet patterned with orange and green, and a settee and two armchairs in the same shade of green. The curtains would be basically oatmeal, boldly patterned in green, brown, orange and yellow. My table, chairs and bedroom furniture would all be in a medium oak—and so the dreams went on. But no flat materialized, and my health deteriorated further while I continued this fruitless search.

I partly cheered myself up by buying some colourful clothes and promptly earned Exclusive Brethren disapproval by wearing a red hat, shoes and gloves to liven up my grey utility coat, but I had become too dispirited to care and ignored their criticism.

The hospital specialist recommended that I should at least have a good holiday. I took his advice and went to Switzerland for three weeks. I knew that running away would not solve my problems, any more than it would have solved the psalmist David's, but what a joyful respite to relax on the shores of Lake Geneva to recharge my batteries!

Maybe I was running away from God too. Despite all my failings towards him, I felt that God had let me down by not answering my fervent prayers for a flat. My weak faith wavered further and I wondered if he really cared about me. I even doubted his power to help anyway, so spiritually low had I sunk.

But my choice of resort proved excellent. Water is a wonderful tranquillizer for a troubled mind and battered emotions. I spent many hours beside the lake, gazing at the swaying willows and drinking in the serenity. I also gained inspiration from the grandeur of the mountains on the far shore as I lazed in the sun.

The Brethren, I knew, would have disapproved of all this admiration of 'fallen nature'. But I did not know that God was close to me, waiting to reveal himself in a new, fresh way.

One hot afternoon I sat on a small landing-stage to dangle my feet in the cool water. A light breeze played with my hair, a pair of swans rippled the water as they glided past, and I felt at peace with all the world.

A sense of foreboding and awareness of change disturbed this peace. An eerie stillness replaced the whisper of the breeze, and even the swans altered their behaviour. They stood in the shallows – alert, expectant.

The light dimmed, the lake turned grey-purple, and several holiday-makers ran for shelter. I looked with apprehension at the darkening sky but decided to stay where I was. A deafening thunderclap followed a brilliant lightning flash, and the storm broke. Lightning ran down the mountainside beyond the lake, thunder roared over-head, but I still sat on the landing-stage, small and insignificant in the drama of the storm.

My spine tingled with awe as a jagged fork of lightning zipped across the water. Torrential rain soaked me in seconds, but this fantastic display was too good to miss.

The lake, previously so calm, whipped itself into a boiling cauldron of fury. Fascinated, I watched the swans face the angry water, rising proudly on the crest of the inky waves. A little voice within whispered that I ought to face my challenges like that too, but I did not want to hear it.

The storm abated as suddenly as it began, and I regretted that the drama had played itself out so soon. God had shared a spectacular display of his power, and it left me deeply moved.

There was I, so frail and weak, but the God of the storm chose to reveal his might to me. This was the God I had largely ignored for too long, and had deemed too small to solve my problems.

Did he use the storm to chastise my lack of true Christian commitment and weak faith? Shame filled me, and yet I did not want to feel like that. I longed for a close personal relationship with God once more, and to know his presence more intimately than in the sharing of that sudden tempest.

The clouds moved to the slopes at the end of the lake, where they hung like heavy, black curtains. The sun shone again, turning the raindrops into diamonds. And then I saw the rainbow! I gazed spellbound, and a half-remembered verse from the Bible sprang to mind: 'I set my bow in the cloud ...'. My heart overflowed with wonder and praise.

I had dreaded returning from that holiday, but felt assured that God would help me. The God behind the thunderstorm could do anything! Previously I had limited him by equating his power with human ability and made him a thousand thunderstorms too small. It took only one to show me how great he really is.

A few days later I came home. The lake, the mountains, the beauty and peace, were all left behind, but I felt much better for those blissful three weeks. They were not long enough to undo the strain of years, but they provided a wonderful respite.

Once home the pressures soon weighed heavily again. My parents either shouted at each other, or ignored each other, and I felt a nonentity in their eyes. Bitterness and recriminations remained the order of my home-life. How much longer could I stand it? How could I escape with nowhere to go?

My search for a flat continued. Flats to rent were an almost unheard-of luxury after the war and I had insufficient money to buy one.

My health and morale reached an all-time low and the hospital specialist became more insistent about the urgency of leaving home. I fell beside my bed in an agony of prayer: 'Please, Lord, help me!' In my dilemma Lake Geneva, the mountains, the thunderstorm and my awareness of God seemed all too remote and irrelevant to my plight.

My God had become too small again. Would he drop a flat down from heaven by parachute just for me? The very thought seemed irreverent and my head dropped onto the bed in despair.

The Exclusive Brethren elders reprimanded me for my 'worldliness' in going to Switzerland on a pleasure-seeking holiday (they went abroad only to 'encourage the saints they visited'), but I hardly listened. Neither did I explain my reason for going. I felt too weary to bother and other problems concerned me more than their adverse criticisms.

One evening I went round to Lillian's house to pour out my troubles. She had assured me many times that God had a plan for my life which he would reveal step by step, but I had been walking this same dreary, hate-ridden stretch of road for so long.

This time Lillian said something different: 'You know, Christine, it may be that God won't lead you to another home just because you *want* to go. He will move you when you really *need* to go.'

'But the specialist insists that I need to go now,' I protested.

To my dismay Lillian went on to suggest that God might never move me. Instead he would give me the grace and strength to overcome the friction and coldness. She urged me to be willing to stay and be strengthened.

Although an undertow of fear tugged at my heart, yet God reached me through Lillian's words. He continued the message he had begun while I sat beside that Swiss lake. He wanted me to be willing to stay and face up to the storm, as those swans had done – and he would reveal more of himself through my difficulties. I would forfeit this awareness if I took fright and fled.

I wrestled with God that night but ended up willing to stay at home if he would strengthen me. Instead of struggling and striving, I laid my burden at his feet and left it there. Deep, refreshing sleep followed, such as I had not known for weeks. Peace still remained when, some days later, I had a telephone call at the office from the jovial, friendly man who had been deputy to my boss.

Big-hearted Mr Edgar had been most considerate to me before a heart condition forced him into early retirement. He often allowed his secretary to help me code long, secret cables to the firm's overseas branches. In return I typed his letters when she was ill or on holiday.

Sometimes I talked to Mr Edgar about my personal problems in a way that I would not have dreamed of doing to my own austere boss. Mr Edgar knew of my longing for my own home and once told me that he wished he could offer me one of the flats he had bought in Brighton.

'The trouble is they're rent-controlled. This means I can't give the tenants notice, but if one leaves you'll get first option on the flat, Mr Edgar told me.

I knew this was a genuine promise but the chance of Mr Edgar being able to keep it appeared remote. People just did not vacate rent-controlled flats in those days. It provided a straw to cling to but when Mr Edgar retired I gave up hope. Why should he remember me?

Then came that Friday telephone call.

'Still looking for a flat?' Mr Edgar asked.

'Y-yes,' I faltered.

'Well, one of mine's vacant. The old girl cleared out yesterday. Come and see it tomorrow. If you like it, it's yours. Are you interested?'

Was I! I managed to stammer that I would come down the next morning, then felt horribly sick. After all the years of searching this must be too good to be true. I had not seriously considered living as far from London as Brighton, but why not? Mr Edgar had travelled up daily after he bought the flats, so why shouldn't I?

My heart thumped as I rang Mr Edgar's doorbell. His round, apple-red face broke into a beaming smile when he opened the door. He welcomed me into his stately old house, which had been divided into five flats, and led me to the white, panelled door at the far end of the spacious hall.

'Your front door, my dear,' he said, flinging it open.

I stepped into a huge bed-sitting room and loved it on sight. The large bay window looked onto trees that shone like burnished gold and bronze in the autumn sunshine. The kitchen shared the same view, and the bathroom overlooked next door's rose garden.

'It's marvellous! Fantastic!' I exclaimed.

I arranged for the flat to be redecorated, which it badly needed, and enjoyed myself buying the furnishings. Mrs Edgar came shopping with me and her sister-in-law made my curtains.

I moved in on a beautiful, late autumn day, greeted by the roaring fire that my landlord had kindly lit. My eyes misted over at the sight of the beige carpet patterned in orange and green, and the three piece suite in the same shade of green. I blinked at the medium oak table and chairs, the bed tucked away in the far corner and the 'utility' oak wardrobe to match.

My feet sank into the carpet as I crossed to the window and looked across the valley to the gold and bronze-leafed trees beyond, while my fingers caressed the oatmeal curtains boldly patterned in green, brown, orange and yellow.

Mr Edgar tactfully left me standing there, too overcome for words. My dream had at last come true and I felt as if a little bit of heaven had come to earth for me. It would take only a rainbow to arc across the sky to complete the picture. Yet the picture was complete without it, since a rainbow encircled my heart instead.

Of course God loved me! Of course he cared! He had been with me in the storm. He knew how much I could take and came to my help with the most perfect timing once I lay my burden at his feet. I was beginning to rediscover what David affirmed so long ago: 'My times are in thy hands'. I only regret that I foolishly snatched so much time back to spend in my own misguided ways.

Chapter Five

Recovery from burnout is a slow and painful process, especially when 'nervous colitis' also strikes. My burnout certainly did not disappear overnight, although having my own home did wonders for my morale. For many weeks my peaceful, cosy flat so delighted me that I spent most of my spare time within its four walls. I had no local friends, other than my landlord and his wife, but that did not worry me.

Once energy returned, I enjoyed exploring the neighbourhood. Nearby Preston Park often lured me to its green pleasantness and I looked forward to the spring, when Mr Edgar told me it would be ablaze with flowers of every hue.

Despite two long train journeys and tiring days at the office, my health continued to improve. My landlord took a fatherly interest in my well-being, a welcome new experience. He encouraged me to enjoy the sea breezes along the sea front at weekends. Had he been a fitter man he would probably have come with me, but I liked going alone. The cries of the gulls and the sight and sound of waves crashing on the pebbles were new to me and I loved them.

The fresh, tangy air and bracing walks to Hove and back did more for my physical well-being than any tonic. As I felt the caress of the sea air on my face, I often had a greater awareness of God's tenderness and nearness. I was learning that he 'makes everything beautiful in its time', as that wise man Solomon knew, and that God was doing a new thing in my life. I needed only to await his timing, not an easy thing to do with my impatient, stubborn nature.

With the physical build-up, my mental and emotional scars also began to heal and my spirits revived. I felt motivated once more and took up knitting, embroidery and rug making. I enjoyed these quiet but creative pursuits while sitting beside my coal fire, with its warming, cheery flames.

In my daily travel to work I made friends with Beryl, Marion and Gillian, three other regulars on the 8.10 to Victoria. Beryl loved wide open spaces and, as our friendship deepened, we went on many long, wintry walks across the Downs and up to Devil's Dyke.

After I had been in Brighton for several weeks I also ran into Anna, one of my Exclusive friends.

'What are you doing here, and where have you been for so long?' she asked in surprise.

We sat in a shelter on the front, where I explained that I now had my own flat near Preston Park.

'My parents live in Hove and I've come home to look after my sick mother,' Anna told me.

We talked for a long time and she urged me to link up with the Exclusive Brethren again.

'Don't forget that the assembly is the true Pauline church, the Bride of Christ,' Anna cautioned. 'If you join a Petrine church, that's only the world's system of religion and, as we know, that's all counterfeit.'

I had been away from Exclusive teaching and language for so many weeks that it sounded strange to hear someone talking like this again. While Anna chattered on I tried to work out in my mind the difference between churches founded by Paul and Peter.

'Do write to the meeting in Surrey and ask for a letter of commendation to the saints here,' Anna urged, interrupting my thoughts. 'They'll be pleased to hear from you after the way you suddenly disappeared.'

'I don't know that they will. They may feel I've let them down,' I hedged.

'One or two brothers called at your parents' home, you know, but they couldn't find out where you were. Why didn't you tell us you were moving?'

Anna's solemn grey eyes showed genuine hurt and concern and I felt mean at departing so secretly. Yet, even as I went on the defensive to give a satisfactory explanation, I knew I was beginning to change. I had become tired of the Brethren making so many decisions for me. For once I had been determined to take full responsibility for my own action of moving to Brighton.

All the same that unexpected meeting with Anna unsettled me. It brought to the surface a build-up of guilt over my lack of Christian fellowship. Once or twice I had looked longingly at the young people chatting outside a large, grey stone church near my flat. I had felt tempted to join them but the Exclusive insistence that 'we are the only ones who are right' held me back. In Brethren terms, I still wanted to be a 'Philadelphian Christian' (the ones in Revelation in whom Christ had nothing to condemn) and not a Laodicean one (lukewarm, blind and abhorrent to Christ).

Eventually a longing for Christian fellowship motivated me to write for a letter of commendation, as Anna had urged, yet inwardly I vowed never again to allow the Exclusives to dominate my thought patterns, nor would I allow them to make decisions for me to the same extent.

My request for this letter must have caused a stir in my home town for some senior brothers and their wives promptly drove to Brighton to see me. They rebuked me for not informing them of my move and I showed due contrition for my independent action.

After further reprimands, apologies and forgiveness, the Brethren settled down to a picnic supper which they had brought with them. They then requested me to put a hat on so that they could pray for me. (A brother will not pray in the presence of a sister unless she covers her head.)

Had I received the Brethren's rebukes in a rebellious spirit, they would not have eaten in my flat but would have kept their picnic for the roadside. As it was, a letter of commendation duly came and I presented myself at the local assembly. They received me into fellowship, but soon reprimanded me for wearing a gold locket and chain and high-heeled shoes.

Despite my worldly weaknesses, I made several friends among the younger members of both the Brighton and Hove assemblies and enjoyed inviting them to my flat. It did a lot for my self-esteem to entertain in this way, since I had never been allowed to do so when living with my parents. Anna came most frequently and I remember showing her a Fair Isle sweater I had just completed and a rug still in the making.

'I love the jumper but of course I wouldn't dare to wear anything so brightly coloured,' Anna sighed.

She also admired my embroidered tablecloth and stroked the woolly rug.

'How clever you are!' she exclaimed. 'I'm horribly unproductive, but with so many meetings to attend and Mother to care for, there's no time for anything creative. Meetings have always dominated my life.'

I felt sorry for the rigid upbringing that forced Anna to attend everything the Brethren arranged and became even more determined that they would never have such a stranglehold on me. I went to the meetings I wanted to attend but absented myself from the rest. I just could not face dreary week night meetings after a gruelling day at the office.

Despite these reservations, I did make some attempt to live up to Brethren expectations. But my new navy blue coat and pudding-bowl hat served only to hide the real me needing to escape.

In my desire to be accepted by the Brighton Exclusives, I once again substituted a legal code of Thou Shalt Nots for a true personal relationship with God. Because this spiritual decline was subtle and gradual, I failed to recognize what had happened.

'You talk about Jesus as if you knew him personally,' an elderly sister said wistfully. 'It takes me so much time and effort to get to the various meetings that any kind of private prayer life or communion with God gets pushed aside.'

I should have heeded the veiled warning in this remark. Instead I became so enmeshed in the Exclusive system again that I ignored all inner promptings to walk with God and not before men.

In a way I led a kind of Jekyll and Hyde existence and felt a different, more liberated person when out with Beryl and my two other 'worldly' friends. Sometimes I also found it fun to break the rules with less dedicated Exclusive friends, although these escapades (all very innocent really) left me with a nagging sense of failure.

Why stay with the Exclusives if you can't be whole-hearted about it, I asked myself - and felt a hypocrite as well as a failure. Where was I heading? What was my true motive? I hardly knew. But I did know that I needed someone somewhere to accept me, just as I was deep within and not the surface me who wore a 'go to meeting' face on Sundays.

For months the doubts niggled, not only about my own position, but also about the bizarre Exclusive teaching and fanciful interpretations of biblical prophecy that had begun to invade the 'assembly'.

I rarely shared my doubts, even with my broader-minded Exclusive friends, yet they had an uncomfortable way of continually resurfacing, like sharp-toothed rocks that emerge and disappear with the ebb and flow of the tide.

Fortunately God's gaze penetrates right through our facades. He knew my deepest heart longings, but was prepared to wait until I faced up to my stubbornness and pride, just as the father waited for his wayward son in the immortal story that Jesus told. Then, and only then, would he do a new thing in my life and I, in the words of Paul's letter to the Ephesians, would no longer be a spiritual infant 'tossed back and forth by the waves, and blown here and there by every wind of teaching ...'.

While either battling with, or trying to ignore, my doubts about the rightness of remaining with the Exclusive Brethren, a 'weak' sister gave me a book.

'It's written by a Quaker, dear, but I believe it will help you,' this motherly lady whispered. 'You won't betray me for giving it to you, will you?'

I promised to be discreet and *The Christian's Secret of a Happy Life* by Hannah Pearsall Smith became my prized companion on many a train journey. So much of that book met my need that I am certain God moved the donor to buy it for me. My mind whirled with uncertainty and confusion as I read: 'Many earnest and honest-hearted children of God have been deluded into paths of extreme fanaticism, while all the while thinking they were closely following the Lord. God, who sees the sincerity of their hearts, can and does, I am sure, pity and forgive ...'. I just couldn't get those words out of my mind, they so exactly described my position. I also admitted that I was not closely following the Lord, who had less and less place in my life. My struggle to please men rather than God left me bewildered and disillusioned. Yet deep within a heart hunger remained for a fresh assurance of God's love for, and approval of, me personally.

'You need to be careful ...', Mrs Green had wisely advised years before, but I had not listened. Instead I had entrusted my spiritual direction to people who, however well-meaning, failed to understand the clear teaching of God's Word.

'Why did God allow me to join the Exclusives if it was all a ghastly mistake?' I asked Mrs Hammond, who had given me the book. 'He knew I was sincere in my motives.'

'Beyond knowing that God respects our free will, I can't answer that, dear,' Mrs Hammond replied, 'but I do sympathize with you. As you know, my own loyalties are divided between my own side of the family, who are all Exclusives, and my Anglican husband. He can't stand Brethren dogmatism and legality and so I'm in a cleft stick.'

In my mounting anguish I at last sought God's face about my plight. 'Lord, I've made a bad choice in the leaders I've followed,' I confessed. 'I'm sorry for my wilfulness. Please forgive me and send someone into my life who will help me to do the right thing.'

In my impatient way I expected an instant answer, forgetting that God works to his own time schedule and that sometimes his answer is Wait.

'Lord, who will you send? And when?' became my daily heart cry.

Chapter Six

While I was still praying for guidance, or for the strength to do what I knew in my heart to be right, a new accountancy clerk joined the firm where I worked. I came to know Geoffrey Wood well by sight, even admired his black, wavy hair, but I had no reason to speak to him. It certainly did not cross my mind that he would be God's answer to my prayers for help.

One Monday morning an older clerk burst into my office with the latest news.

'Guess what? You know that chap Wood? Well he got converted over the weekend. You and he should get on fine!' he beamed.

'What do you mean, converted?' I asked cautiously.

'You know - SAVED!' the clerk grinned. 'It happened at All Souls Church in Langham Place. Ask him yourself if you don't believe me. He can't stop talking about it.'

This news so thrilled me that I wanted to rush off and tell Geoffrey Wood how pleased I was to hear of his new-found faith in Christ. Only one thing held me back. The Exclusives had recently intensified their 'separation' teaching and had challenged me because I had been seen out with Beryl and Marion. I had slight pangs of conscience about my friendship with these two but appeased them by resolving to form no more 'outside links' while

I remained with the Exclusive Brethren.

All unknowingly, Geoffrey Wood put my resolution to the test and I questioned the rightness of this strict separation doctrine. The more I thought and prayed about it, the more convinced I became that God wanted me to build bridges instead of walls; to reach out to those beyond the Exclusive boundary, instead of remaining so insulated. Further, I must not allow the Brethren to make decisions for me again.

A few days later Geoffrey walked towards me as I went out to lunch. I took a deep breath and plunged in.

'Excuse me, but I hear you've recently become a Christian. I'm so pleased,' I said.

His whole face glowed and I knew I had done the right thing in speaking to him. Geoffrey told me how lonely he had been that life-changing Sunday, and how he had gone to All Souls when someone had handed him an invitation card to the evening service. He had listened enthralled to a sermon on the woman at Sychar's well and before the service ended, the Saviour who had touched that sinful woman's heart had touched Geoffrey's heart too.

We had so much to say, but Geoffrey's lunch hour had ended. I told him where to find my office and he became a regular visitor. I mentioned that I was an Exclusive sister but this meant nothing to Geoffrey as he had never heard of this sect. I on the other hand recoiled when he invited me to All Souls. An Anglican church! Part of the world's religious system! The Sardis of Revelation three - according to the Exclusives!

'I'd like you to hear John Stott. He's a marvellous preacher,' Geoffrey enthused.

My refusal to come puzzled him, although I did my best to explain. My mind reeled in confusion. If I left the Exclusives, I would have to go somewhere for Christian fellowship. What *did* I want?

'I can't understand why you won't come when John Stott's such a super Christian,' Geoffrey frowned, and the confusion was mutual.

Despite this bad start, our friendship grew and more and more I came to see what a stranglehold the Exclusive Brethren had on me. I had become far more fettered than I realised, but Geoffrey - a new, young Christian - took upon himself the task of setting me free. The timing of God's answer to my prayers for help could not have been more perfect, yet how humbling that he used a new convert to do the job!

Geoffrey loved cycling and often set off early to spend Saturdays with me in Brighton. We also spent happy evenings together in London when night school studies allowed him to. Our friendship deepened and Geoffrey often said that he wished I did not live so far away.

'Why don't you move nearer to London?' he suggested.

'I wouldn't be able to get a rent-controlled flat,' I told him.

'But rents are likely to be decontrolled soon anyway,' Geoffrey warned me.

A few weeks later my kindly landlord died of a heart

61

attack. All his tenants loved him and his passing distressed us. Perhaps I missed him most. Mr Edgar had been a real father to me, the only father I had known.

Mrs Edgar went to her sister in Scotland after the funeral and everything changed. My flat lost its charm and I felt restless and insecure. My disillusionment with the Exclusives also grew as they brought in more bizarre doctrine and practices. I had nothing against my personal friends among them, and loved my 'second mum' Mrs Hammond. I distrusted and disliked the tyrannical system that now forbade personal friendships in the assembly in favour of relating to all the brethren on an equal footing. I also refused to wear a bow, or 'token' in my hair as a 'mark of submission'.

One weekend I made a rare visit to my parents. On the way from the station I saw a new block of flats. It so excited me that I jumped off the bus at the next stop and hurried back to the site.

'They're all sold, love,' the foreman told me, as I peered through a flat window, 'but we're building another block down the side road. They'll sell quickly too, being so close to the station. If you're interested, nip down to the Estate Agent right away.'

Why not buy a flat? A mortgage would probably cost no more than a decontrolled rent and I would possess something for the money. I went to the Estate Agent for full details, and he showed me a plan of the new block.

'I'll have this centre flat with the bay window,' I said. 'Will you reserve it for me?'

I knew nothing whatever about buying property, deposits, mortgages or surveyors' fees but I soon learned. The deposit presented no problem as I had always been thrifty, but the mortgage proved another story. The Estate Agent offered to arrange one but I politely refused, preferring to make my own arrangements.

One Building Society after another turned me down and I learned the hard way that they regarded single women unfavourably. In my determination to get a mortgage from one society I applied to two of its branches and finally direct to their Head Office - all to no avail.

I swallowed my pride and returned to the Estate Agent, who repeated his offer of arranging one. He obtained a mortgage for me from the very society that had turned me down three times! I had a lot to learn about 'pulling the right strings'.

The following Monday Geoffrey returned from a fortnight's holiday. He overtook me on Waterloo Bridge and I excitedly told him my news.

'I've bought a flat,' I announced.

'Bought one!' he exclaimed.

He said little then but later told me that he wished I had not been so impetuous.

'You're a funny mixture,' he said. 'You cling to those Brethren with whom you're not really happy, yet you rush off to buy a flat without thinking twice about it.'

A smile crinkled the corners of his greyish-green eyes, yet the disappointment in his voice sent my spirits plummeting.

'What's wrong with buying a flat?' I asked.

'Just this. I want to marry you and it would have been much nicer to choose a home together,' he said, his eyes searching mine.

My thoughts churned again. Mrs Hammond had married an Anglican and never lived down the 'disgrace'. But that was amongst the Exclusive Brethren ... and I wanted to sever my links, didn't I? *Did I or didn't I?* I had sat on the fence for so long that it exasperated even me.

I stared at Geoffrey, my emotions in a turmoil. He held my hands in his and looked at me questioningly. In that moment I knew I loved him, and told him so.

'No one's going to keep us apart,' I promised myself.

Geoffrey wanted us to become engaged at once but I hedged for time.

'I'm going to be disloyal to some good friends and can't just walk out on them,' I explained.

'Say goodbye to them when you leave Brighton and we'll become engaged then,' Geoffrey suggested.

Looking back, I marvel at his patience, understanding and tolerance.

A few months later I moved into the new flat and Geoffrey and I became engaged. A completely new horizon opened up before me and I felt happier than I dreamed possible.

My new home stood bathed in September sunshine and I loved its brightness. Geoffrey cycled over to help me get it straight by making pelmets, putting up shelves and curtains and laying carpets. As we worked together I wished we were already married. And we could have been, had my sense of loyalty to Exclusive friends not hindered us. Although I had been so slow in shaking off Brethren fetters, now I could hardly wait to marry the man I loved.

'How foolish to tie yourself to a *man* when you have such a well-paid job and can support yourself,' my mother said scathingly, when I told her of my forthcoming marriage.

She said a great deal more, from which I gleaned that love did not enter into her thinking. I saw no point in arguing, so Geoffrey and I went ahead with our wedding plans, in which neither of my parents took any interest.

I had been away from 'the world's religious system' for so long that I could not face a church wedding, especially without parental support. I loved Geoffrey even more for his sympathetic understanding of my problem.

'How do the Exclusives marry?' he asked.

'In a Registry office, to comply with the law of the land,' I told him.

So we decided on a quiet Registry office wedding with two of Geoffrey's friends as our witnesses. Since we married in January, we had only a weekend honeymoon in London with the promise of a second honeymoon in the summer. On the Sunday we attended All Souls Church, where John Stott prayed with us and gave a private blessing on our marriage. We appreciated that as we wanted God to be at the helm as we embarked upon our life together.

Geoffrey also wanted us to make a fresh beginning so he left All Souls and we attended a local Baptist Church. Although a strange, new experience for both of us, we received a warm welcome, which helped us to settle down.

Geoffrey studied books on basic Christian truths, while I had much to relearn and a lot of false teaching to unlearn. This gave us a spiritual oneness which we treasured.

My spiritual outlook had become so confined, and my vision of what God wanted to do in my life so dimmed that I needed to expand my horizon. God had many precious things to reveal about himself and his ways but, as I discovered, the learning would prove costly.

****

Compared with many others, my severance from the Exclusive Brethren proved easier than I had dared to hope. Withdrawers who are born into the sect suffer from many a nervous breakdown, much false guilt and other intense suffering caused by their utter rejection. Fortunately I was spared all that.

After informing the local assembly of my marriage, I simply received notice of a Care Meeting convened to consider my case. I did not attend, but subsequently received the following withdrawal letter from a senior Brother:

Dear Mrs Wood,

It is with great sorrow of heart that I have to inform you that, at the meeting of assembly character held last evening (of which you were advised) it was decided that, in view of the mixed marriage you have now contracted with one not walking in the light of Paul's ministry (to whom was committed the light of the assembly), we can no longer walk with you. For your information the scriptures read and considered were: Nehemiah 13: 23-26 and 2 Timothy 2: 19-22. Yours faithfully,

....

Free at last! Free to rediscover that life includes bright colours - red, yellow, orange, green and blue as well as the all too familiar black, navy blue, dark greys and browns to which I had become accustomed. More important, I regained a personal relationship with God, the God of love, mercy and forgiveness.

Chapter Seven

With Geoffrey I rediscovered much that I had forgotten - the delight of walking barefoot on dew soaked grass; the scent of wild roses and meadowsweet and the sound of bees buzzing amongst clover. I listened with newly attuned ears to the rapturous song of a mistle thrush welcoming the burgeoning of new springtime beginnings. I also recalled with sadness the time I walked home with an Exclusive brother. On the way I had paused to admire two almond trees.

'Just look at that pink blossom. Isn't it beautiful?' I had enthused.

'I'm dead to all that, dear sister,' this sombre-faced man had replied.

I felt crushed, soul-chilled, but later I also tried to ignore such things. In so doing I drew further away from the God who created such loveliness. But now I could luxuriate once again in nature's riotous bounty and experience the inner joy of being more fully alive. And I didn't even feel guilty about it!

God, I learned, is forever willing to offer us a new beginning. He gave the apostle Paul a fresh start on the Damascus Road which changed his life completely. Less dramatically, he did a new thing in my life when I left the Exclusive Brethren.

Geoffrey and I both loved the country and we enjoyed long walks together whenever we had a free Saturday. Geoffrey never set off without a folding saw in his rucksack. When we came to a tree strangled by ivy he would stop, take out his little saw and cut through the offending creeper. He cared about overgrown footpaths too, and we spent many hours clearing the footpaths of Surrey. Somehow I did not mind being stung by nettles or scratched by brambles. It was all part of Geoffrey's good cause.

One sun-kissed, spring day we climbed over an old stone wall and found ourselves on a mossy path arched by yew and giant laurel bushes. Silence reigned along this vaulted path. No bird sang, no breeze whispered among the laurel leaves. We trod silently, spoke only in whispers, and wondered where the path would lead us. Suddenly it opened on to a grass bank where hundreds of golden daffodils welcomed us. We stood motionless, hand-in-hand, awestruck by this sight, so golden, and so unexpected.

Only one thing marred the beauty. Brambles choked many of the daffodils, others reached for daylight among a forest of silver birch and sycamore saplings. I knew exactly what Geoffrey would do. He ran down the bank, saw in hand, and began cutting away the brambles. I wished I had a saw too. I sat on the bank and watched Geoffrey tenderly lifting first one and then another deformed stalk, gently coaxing the flower it bore towards the sunlight - and I loved him for it.

As I gazed up at the cloudless sky and watched sunbeams dancing among the beech leaves overhead, the words of Psalm Eight, which I learned in my Crusader days, came to mind vibrant with fresh meaning. David's heart must have overflowed with awe and wonder as he sang : 'O LORD, our Lord, how excellent is thy name in all the earth! ... when I consider thy heavens, the work of thy fingers, the moon and the stars ... what is man ...?'

I felt an affinity with David as I looked with new awareness at the beauty surrounding me. My heart also rejoiced in God's loving care and patience despite all my folly and failure.

****

Our first busy, happy years of marriage quickly passed. I continued to work full-time as well as running our home. Geoffrey spent his evenings either at night school or in the flat studying for his accountancy exams. I loved to watch him filling up page after page with his small, neat handwriting. Sometimes I lightly caressed his thick, wavy hair as he pored over his books, but we seldom spoke. That would have interrupted his train of thought.

Once my household tasks were done, I needed something to occupy myself. I had always been interested in writing and began to write stories for children's annuals. I sat on the floor, pencil and paper at the ready as I gazed into the fire. Some evenings ideas flowed, at other times inspiration eluded me, but I enjoyed those quiet, creative hours spent either scribbling or thinking as I watched the dancing flames.

The more I got to know Geoffrey, the more my love grew. I admired his meticulous care in all he did. I learned how sensitive his nature was and how deeply he felt about many things. Not a man to seek the limelight, Geoffrey loved to serve and work behind the scenes. And he did everything well, whether at home, at church or in the office. Daily I thanked God for my kind, wise, and dependable husband. After all the lonely years, it meant more than I could say to have such a loving, understanding companion.

Geoffrey passed his elementary and intermediate accountancy exams and we rejoiced over these successes. I pursued my writing interests while he continued to study but we looked forward to final success when we would spend more time together in shared interests. We seldom listened to the radio, had no television, but derived satisfaction from our achievements.

During our third year together Geoffrey persuaded me to enter a competition by writing a twelve-part children's serial. His pride and delight when my entry won first prize filled me with such encouragement and enthusiasm that I felt I could write a best-seller (not that I ever did). But it felt good to see that serial unfold in print month by month.

Annual holidays always highlighted our years, and we eagerly planned and saved for them. We had no car but Geoffrey enjoyed driving so we hired one and drove off to the West Country. One summer we toured north Devon and Cornwall, returning along the south coast. On the way

I mentioned Mrs Green, my former Crusader leader.

'She and her husband retired to Combe Martin after the war. It would be lovely to see her again,' I said wistfully.

'What's her address?' Geoffrey asked.

'When I write to her I simply put "Trees", Combe Martin,' I said.

'No road?' Geoffrey asked in surprise.

'No, but my letters get there,' I replied, and Geoffrey shrugged.

A few days later we drove down the steep main street of a small Devonian town.

'This is Combe Martin, but how do we find a house called "Trees?"' Geoffrey grinned.

I had no idea where we were and looked out of the car window in surprise. A moment later I could hardly believe my eyes.

'There's Mrs Green going into that baker's shop!' I exclaimed.

I scrambled out of the car and ran to the shop. Sure enough, there stood Mrs Green, elderly, white-haired and leaning on a walking stick, but it overjoyed me to see her. I waited until she had been served with sandwiches, then asked her if she recognized me.

'Christine! Well I never!' she cried, and the delight I felt when she kissed me still warms my heart when I think of it.

More than sixteen years had passed since she wished me a sad farewell from Crusaders. I had written occasionally and, more latterly, had sent her copies of the various Scripture Union and other magazines for which I wrote.

'My husband and I are having a picnic on the sand. Do join us,' Mrs Green invited.

I bought some sandwiches and Geoffrey drove us down to the beach. We had so much to say to each other that we could hardly eat.

'I enjoy the stories and articles you send me,' Mrs Green said. 'I've noticed a gradual improvement in your style. Keep it up.'

'I intend to,' I assured her.

'If God had told me when I started the Crusader Class that one of my girls would become a writer for him, I wouldn't have believed it,' she went on.

Her words touched me deeply. Even when in the Exclusives I longed to write but, like any form of public speaking, such an activity by a 'sister' would have been frowned upon, since ours was a passive, submissive role.

'I wish I hadn't wasted so much time,' I said.

Even as I spoke, the years fell away and I saw myself as a seventeen-year-old girl again. Vividly I recalled that evening when I prayed from a full heart: 'O Lord, make me like Mrs Green'. Maybe God had wanted to answer that prayer for a long time but my stubbornness and pride had blocked the way. Once I confessed my mistake and left the Exclusives, God blessed me by answering that prayer. He had answered abundantly, too, since I could reach more children with my pen than Mrs Green ever could in her class. Although I did not know it that day on the beach, God would go on answering in other ways beyond my imagination.

A lump rose in my throat as I savoured a moment of sheer happiness. Too choked to speak, I could only watch white-frilled waves playfully slapping the limpet-covered rocks as I marvelled yet again at God's patience with me.

I never saw Mrs Green again for she died a few months later in her eighty-fifth year, but I will always be grateful to God for his gracious timing of our meeting on that sunny day in Devon.

****

That reunion with Mrs Green stirred a desire deep within which I believe the Holy Spirit nudged to the surface as a further answer to my youthful prayer.

'I'd love to teach at Crusaders,' I told Geoffrey on our return from that holiday.

He encouraged me to phone the present leader, who I had known from our own Girl Crusader days.

'You couldn't have phoned at a better time,' Marjorie enthused. 'We urgently need a junior teacher since Susan left to get married.'

So I became an Assistant Leader at our local class. An overwhelming sense of awe swept over me as I taught fourteen eight and nine-year olds. Was I really becoming that much like Mrs Green?

In the weeks that followed doubts arose since Mrs Green had always appeared so calm and relaxed. If God was answering my girlhood prayer, I still had a long way to go. When leaving the Exclusive Brethren I thought I had escaped with a minimum of emotional distress. Now I discovered my mistake.

Sunday by Sunday symptoms similar to my old illness returned. I had been passive and inactive for so long that it proved hard to cope with this new experience. I struggled to overcome my nervousness at speaking to the girls, but with little success. In the end I went to the doctor, whose daughter attended my class.

'You mean you're afraid of little girls like this?' the kindly doctor asked, pulling forward a framed photograph of his bright-eyed, blonde-plaited eight-year old.

He reluctantly gave me a few tranquillizers but assured me that the only way to overcome my 'panic attacks' was to keep on teaching. *Had Mrs Green ever felt like this?* I wondered.

'I used to be scared of public speaking,' the doctor sympathized, 'but I stuck at it until now I can do it with ease.'

His words encouraged me and slowly I overcame this hang-up enough to enjoy the task to which God had called me. But, keen as I was to teach, I still had a lot to learn about claiming Christ's strength in weakness.

Also, I soon found that being a Crusader leader involved more than just teaching fourteen lively girls. We had Crusader outings, for instance. The girls loved them, but I came home exhausted. Then we had Friday games in the recreation ground, when we teachers got to know the children better and took a personal interest in each one. An excellent idea, but I begrudged the time involved as I wanted to be with Geoffrey.

The girls were sorry when early darkness put an end to the games, but it pleased me.

As it turned out, mine was but a short-lived freedom. Hardly, it seemed, had games evenings ended than we began rehearsing a Nativity play to which the girls' parents would be invited.

I tried to show some enthusiasm but once again wished that rehearsals did not take up so much time. Then, the week before Christmas, the Crusader Leader dropped a minor bomb. She told me teachers usually gave each child in their class a small Christmas gift.

'Oh dear!' I inwardly sighed, 'that means fourteen extra presents to rush around for.'

Actually one hasty trip to Woolworth's produced the lot, much to my relief.

The girls were so excited on the Sunday before Christmas that I found it hard work to hold their attention while I talked about the True Meaning of Christmas. By the end of the class the girls had become almost too excited and fidgety to control.

'Stay in your places a minute longer. I've something for each of you to open on Christmas Day,' I said, and bestowed crayons, sugar mice, or golden coins with chocolate insides on each waiting child.

That done I dismissed the class and began to pack up.

'Please, Miss, this is for you,' said a shrill voice, and

Paula handed me a gaily wrapped packet.

Several other girls surprised me by producing packages from the depths of their pockets.

'Open them now, Miss,' encouraged Jane, so I sat down and undid the carefully tied bows.

When I saw the contents of these little parcels tears stung behind my eyes: a hand-painted calendar, a carefully sewn felt comb case, a knitted kettle holder, a neatly woven raffia mat.

'You haven't opened m...mine,' the curly-haired Andrea stuttered shyly.

We unearthed her present from beneath some wrapping paper and she watched me open it with eager eyes. Inside I found a long, wavy strip of red plastic with a mouth and two eyes painted at one end.

'It's a b...book m...marker. It's m....meant to be a b...bookworm,' Andrea said, studying my face anxiously.

My throat ached and I felt deeply ashamed. A single, hasty visit to Woolworth's was all I had devoted to searching out my presents for them, just as I had begrudged some of the other time spent on these children. Yet each of them had put patient, loving workmanship into their gifts, thereby giving me something of themselves in the process. And I had had the temerity to talk to them about the True Meaning of Christmas!

I resolved to be more self-giving in the New Year. God had used those children to show me how to be more like Mrs Green!

Chapter Eight

Geoffrey rarely visited my parents since my father ignored him, but on our fourth Christmas Eve together he cycled over to take my mother a present. He found my father seriously ill and my mother too bewildered to cope. Geoffrey immediately took command and had my father admitted into hospital. He died on Boxing Day, still a stranger to both of us. His passing saddened me. Now there could never be a reconciliation between us.

'If only he could have forgiven me for being born,' I sobbed.

'Regrets achieve nothing,' Geoffrey reminded me tenderly.

He held me in his arms, and I knew that pity for that sick, lonely man touched his heart too. On the surface my father's death did not affect me more than that, sparing me the deep grief that many suffer at the loss of a much loved parent.

My mother needed a lot of guidance over business matters. I also helped to clear her house of an accumulation of unwanted items, all of which kept me occupied and stopped me brooding. But it dismayed me when my mother expressed a great liking for our small home and offered us her large house in exchange. We did not want the burden of a four-bedroomed house with big gardens back and front, so we declined.

'Well, if you don't want the house you could sell it and buy somewhere smaller with the money,' my mother suggested.

'Look, when the estate's settled the house will be in your name. You're the one to sell it,' Geoffrey patiently explained. 'You can then buy yourself a small flat.'

'But I like yours. I want to live there,' Mother persisted.

'We don't want to move,' I objected, trying to harden my heart at my mother's pathetic expression.

'I can't cope with the responsibility of owning property,' she went on, her voice plaintive. 'If you'll let me live in your flat I'll give you the money to buy another one. Then, when I die, you can move back if you want to.'

'I wouldn't mind somewhere with bigger rooms,' Geoffrey told me cautiously, so we seriously began to weigh up the pros and cons of my mother's suggestion.

'She'd be comfortable for life and this flat would be easy for her to run,' I weakened.

'It would also be great for us to choose another home together,' Geoffrey added, warming to the idea.

I understood how he felt since it had always rankled with him that I had chosen the flat before we were engaged. But we could do nothing until my mother's house sold, so we left things at that, with nothing definite decided.

When my father's estate was settled, my mother complained bitterly about still living alone in the big house. She repeated her offer of money for another home if we would allow her to live in our bright, sunny flat.

At last we agreed, and she put the house up for sale. We found ourselves an attractive maisonette with bigger rooms situated in a quiet cul-de-sac and convenient for both shops and the station. With the aid of a bank loan we put down a deposit, confidently expecting this to be only a short-term loan until my mother sold her house.

'You aren't moving far away, are you?' she asked, when I told her we had found a nice maisonette.

'No, only about ten minutes walk from the flat,' I assured her.

The next time she came to tea she again expressed concern about how far from her we would be.

'If you fancy a little walk I'll show you where we are moving to,' I offered, and took her to the maisonette on a newly developed site.

When she had sold her house, my mother dropped a bombshell.

'I don't want your flat after all,' she said off-handedly. 'I've bought a maisonette close to yours.'

I could only stare at her, flabbergasted.

'But ... but what about the money you promised us?' I eventually stammered.

'You can't have it. I need it for the maisonette,' she replied smugly.

And that was that. I had never felt so let down in my life and it put Geoffrey and me into a spin. We had just signed the contract on our new home.

'Why did you show your mother where we were

going?' he seethed, and I burst into tears.

Geoffrey could barely contain his disgust at my mother's change of mind and I must admit it did not improve my relationship with her either. In fact it proved quite a strain on my Christian grace when she asked me to help her pack and move.

'Love suffers long and is kind,' Paul wrote long ago. His words not only challenged me, but they helped me to keep on an even keel.

To ease our financial straits, I resigned from my job. By doing this I obtained, not only repayment of my pension fund contributions, but also the firm's contribution of an equal amount. On a grey, overcast November day I also put my spurned little flat up for sale.

'Not a good selling time,' the Estate Agent predicted gloomily. 'No hope of a quick sale, but we'll do our best.'

As it turned out, the flat sold to the second viewers. They were a charming old couple who asked me to visit them when they had moved in. This I did and we became good friends.

'I know we'll be happy here because there's been love in this place,' white-haired Mrs Chine told me on my first visit. 'Yes, there's been love, dear. I can feel it in the atmosphere.'

Her words soothed like a balm and I never once grieved over leaving that cosy flat.

I used my pension fund money to pay the 'window level instalment' for which the builders clamoured, then quickly obtained another post with the proprietors of

Punch. One of the directors engaged me as his personal secretary and at the *Punch* office I discovered how enjoyable one's work could be with a kind, considerate boss who did not expect tomorrow's work to be done yesterday.

My father's death affected me more than I at first realized. The hurt of his rejection and lack of reconciliation sank deeply into my subconscious to resurface while I struggled with the stresses of changing both home and job.

These emotional undercurrents surfaced in the form of doubts and fears. The most sinister doubt attacked the very roots of my faith. If God really loved me, why had he allowed me to be born into such an unhappy, disunited family? Why did he allow me to have a father who ignored me from birth? Why did I have a mother whose word could not be trusted?

Since I could not answer these nagging Whys, I tried to ignore them by filling my days with busyness. I also struggled with bitterness. I knew Christians should not be bitter, but the feeling kept growing.

I worked hard at the office, at home and in the church, but failed to face up to my motive for all this activity. Inevitably I overworked and had to take enforced rests. Then back would rush the doubts, and the whole vicious circle began again.

This ever-turning circle jolted to a standstill when I turned to Mrs Fraser, a wise, elderly Christian friend, for help.

'Why do you overexert yourself like this, my dear?' she asked, her keen eyes searching my face.

I floundered at her direct question and came up with an answer that sounded unconvincing even to me.

'I suppose I want to show God that I love him,' I said.

'I believe it's the other way round,' Mrs Fraser replied. 'I think you're trying to win God's love. I've news for you though. You don't have to strive like this to make him love you. He loves you already, just as you are.'

Her perceptive frankness shattered me yet I rejoiced in the truth of what she said. I faced up to my motives and saw that all this effort had self-interest at its roots. Worse, in the performing of it, I had lost my girlhood vision of a heavenly Father who loved me so much that he sent his Son to die in my place. Instead I had turned him into a harsh taskmaster.

Rather than admit my mistakes, I hedged by confiding to my friend many things that had disturbed my childhood. I intended to further excuse my wrong motives by posing the question that still nagged: If God loves me, why has he allowed so much suffering?

'I grew up amid violent rows and endless, bitter, verbal battles between my parents,' I went on. 'It terrified me when they fought. What I want to know is, if God loves me ...'.

Mrs Fraser forestalled me by cutting in on my half-formed question.

'Isn't God wonderful?' she beamed. 'To think he loved you, and chose carefully the family that would provide the best background to shape you into the person he wants you to be.'

My jaw dropped open in astonishment, and scales fell from my eyes. In one sentence my friend knocked all the 'ifs' out of my doubting heart. Suddenly I saw that God had planned the family into which I had been born. It had not happened by chance or a lapse of oversight on his part, but by his divine appointment.

'"Before I formed you in the womb I knew you, before you were born I set you apart",' my friend quoted from the first chapter of Jeremiah.

I listened spellbound, for she seemed to read my thoughts. I also marvelled at God's grace and mercy in calling me to himself from such a godless background.

And God had indeed been there in my beginnings. I vividly recalled that when I was four years old, my mother had taken me to church for the first time. Not normally a churchgoing woman, she went that Easter Sunday at a neighbour's invitation.

During the service the tune and tender words of *There is a Green Hill Far Away* enchanted me. Later I asked my mother to sing that 'nice song' again. She could only remember:

> 'There was no other good enough
> To pay the price of sin;
> He only could unlock the gate
> Of heav'n and let us in.'

Mother explained that the hymn was about Jesus who died at Easter for everyone's bad deeds. I believed the little that she could tell me, and the chord her words struck in my heart went on vibrating until, at twelve, I heard the gospel explained more fully and responded gladly by accepting Christ as my own personal Saviour.

As I talked to Mrs Fraser about my home-life, it filled me with awe that that first simple belief had never become lost, even in times of deep unhappiness.

What a wonderful heavenly Father I had! And what a tremendous relief that I had no need to struggle for approval, or to seek by long, arduous labour to win his love. It would no longer be a matter of what I could do for God either, but what his Holy Spirit could do through me. Shame mingled with joy. How could I have doubted my heavenly Father, whose acceptance of me is complete in Jesus Christ? I could only praise God as those dreadful doubts left me. What were they but ghostly phantoms that, like morning mist on a summer day, evaporated when bathed in the sunshine of God's love?

Despite my new-found joy and spiritual release, I found that my human father's rejection had still left emotional scars. These too would have to be dealt with before healing could be complete.

For several days, resentment, anger and bitterness all rose to the surface in a whirlpool of emotions too long suppressed. They washed themselves out of my system in a flood of healing tears. When this emotional storm abated, a still, small voice within whispered: What about forgiveness?

God had forgiven my doubts and other failings, yet I had not forgiven my father for the misery he inflicted.

85

Since he was no longer alive I could not go to him with forgiveness, but once I poured out all the hurt to my heavenly Father and asked for his cleansing, I found that only sorrow remained where previously so much resentment and bitterness had festered.

Past circumstances could not be changed, but I thanked God for inner healing and for my own change of heart.

Chapter Nine

Three years passed and once again we packed for a holiday in Devon.

Crash! The sound of shattering tiles awoke me on the morning of our departure.

'How sad, that lovely old house is dying,' I said to Geoffrey, and I got out of bed to look at the mellow-bricked manor beyond the trees at the end of our garden. Already the quaint, twisty chimneys had gone and the demolishers attacked the roof in earnest.

'Soon that house will be no more than a memory to those who've known and loved it,' I grieved.

'Don't be so gloomy,' Geoffrey said, turning over sleepily. 'Write a book about a house that died and give it a happy ending. Then you won't mind about that old place being pulled down.'

No one could equal my husband for positive, practical advice, even when he was half-asleep. And so a book was conceived amid the creak and groan of prised-up rafters.

We had dreadful weather on that holiday, wind that whipped our hair and left us breathless, or slashing rain that soaked us in minutes, yet it proved one of our happiest. We drove eagerly to the holiday flat we had rented overlooking a quaint Devon harbour, where we worked on my third children's book *The House that Died*.

While I plotted and wrote, Geoffrey studied nineteenth century fashions, having bought some books on costume at a second-hand bookshop. He made helpful notes on the various styles, for which I was grateful. Some Victorian gowns awaited discovery in the attics of my 'dying house' and the descriptions had to be accurate.

In this book the heroine's mother died. I did not want her to die, but somehow the book took over and wrote itself. I prayed about that: 'Dear God, it's as if you want me to define clearly what I understand and believe about death and bereavement. Why?' I asked.

God did show me why, but not then. I had to await his timing. But he did give me the energy and skill to finish the book more quickly than the other two.

Geoffrey looked forward to seeing *The House that Died* in print. Since he had done so much research he called it 'our' book and disliked having to wait a year for its publication.

The year passed and once again we went to our Brixham holiday flat. We enjoyed perfect weather and had a wonderful time swimming, hiking, picnicking on Dartmoor and exploring many other beauty spots.

On the last evening we stood on the balcony of our flat to watch the golden sun of fading day. The sea gradually deepened from liquid amber to blood red before our fascinated eyes. Despite the beauty of that sunset a strange melancholy gripped me as we watched. Geoffrey must have sensed my mood, for he put his arms round me, strong and comforting.

'It makes me sad to see the sun go down,' I whispered.

'Why should it? It's only moving towards tomorrow,' Geoffrey replied.

Was it the cool, evening air, or did some inner sense of foreboding make me shiver as we went indoors?

We arrived home on Saturday afternoon, having done some shopping on the way.

'Perhaps the complimentary copies of "our" book came while we were away,' Geoffrey said, but our neighbours soon dashed his hopes. They had taken in no parcels for us.

The next day we went to an after-church fellowship at our friend Norrie's house. Norrie asked me to close the evening with a short epilogue. He suggested that I should speak for a few minutes on my favourite Bible character.

I chose Joseph, who had been a firm favourite since my Crusader days. I briefly related the story of how his jealous brothers threw him into a pit, then hauled him out again only to sell him as a slave to passing traders.

Joseph had good cause to hate those brothers, yet when famine reunited them in Egypt many years later, he showed a lovely spirit of forgiveness. I opened my Bible and read: 'Do not be grieved or angry with yourselves ... for God sent me before you to preserve life ... You meant evil against me, but God meant it for good ...'.

I reminded my friends that we all have trials to face. We can have health or financial reversals. Others can treat us badly or let us down. None of us know what tomorrow will bring, but some crisis could well assail us. God, I said, is more concerned with our reaction to life's knocks than with what actually happens. If someone wrongs us, will we have Joseph's forgiving spirit?

What if grief or tragedy strike? Will we cry:'Why me?' in aggrieved tones, or will we face our crisis courageously? We can either go through it with God's help, showing Joseph's gracious spirit, or we can become vindictive and rebellious, bitter and resentful.

Two days after I had given that epilogue, Geoffrey went into hospital to have an ingrown tooth removed from the roof of his mouth.

'All quite straightforward. I'll just have a sore mouth for a few days,' he assured me.

'I'll come to see you after work tomorrow,' I promised, a promise I was unable to fulfil.

I had just returned from my lunch break when the ward sister telephoned my *Punch* office to tell me that Geoffrey had died under the anaesthetic.

The telephone slipped from my grasp and I stared unseeing out of the window. Surely there must be some mistake! My husband was young and strong and, anyway, tragedies like that happened only to other people. Slowly, the dreadful truth dawned, and horror changed to grief.

An office colleague drove me to the hospital and watched in silent sympathy when the ward sister brought Geoffrey's clothes, his watch, his ring. I signed a form, choked down a cup of sickly sweet tea, and my friend drove me home.

The days that followed are a blurred nightmare of the

mortuary, the Coroner's Court and the Registrar of Death's office. Relatives and friends did all they could to help, and letters of sympathy arrived from far and near.

On the morning of Geoffrey's funeral the postman delivered six complimentary copies of *The House that Died*. Their arrival added to my grief. Why could they not have come a week earlier?

For a while after the funeral I felt too stunned for the tragedy to fully sink in, too shocked for tears. Gradually the nightmare became reality, and many questions crowded into my mind, clamouring for an answer: Why had this devastating loss come to me? Why should such a fit, strong man die in his thirties? How could a God of love allow such a tragedy, leaving as it did so many plans permanently interrupted, and so many dreams shattered?

One particularly bleak morning, when swirling mists of despair obscured my vision, I slowly turned the pages of *The House that Died* and it helped me to find some answers. As I read, assurance came that my husband's death had not taken God by surprise. He had allowed it, and in the writing of this book he had gently prepared me for what was to come. God knew it would help if I already had my thoughts clarified about death.

Yet how that book challenged! Did I honestly believe what I had written? With tear-dimmed eyes I read my own words: 'I remember John telling me of your mother's death, and I grieved for you,' Miss Ormond said (to the heroine). 'And yet, you know, we must try not to question God's ways. It's so much easier if we believe that he makes no mistakes, and that these sad things are allowed for a purpose.'

'What purpose can there be in someone good getting ill and dying?' Helen asked.

'I once felt just as you do,' Miss Ormond replied gently, 'but eventually I came to accept Hugh's death as being like a dark thread in the pattern of my life. I couldn't appreciate it, but God gave me the faith to believe that such darkness had been allowed only to show up a particularly beautiful part of his design.'

Those were the words I had put into Miss Ormond's mouth. Had I written them with integrity? Sincerity?

Geoffrey's death appeared the blackest of threads in the pattern of my life. Had God allowed it to reveal a specially lovely part of his design? If he had, my tear-filled eyes failed to see it. I clung desperately to the belief that Geoffrey had gone to be with God. One day we would meet again, but for now a frowning desolation all but overwhelmed me.

Amid all the heartbreak of those grief-filled days, an inner voice reminded me of my recent words at Norrie's house: 'What if grief or tragedy strike?' They had struck, but could I display Joseph's lovely spirit, or would I be bitter and resentful? I was deeply conscious that the group to whom I had spoken would be looking at me. Amidst all the emotional buffeting, what would they see? What would they hear? A song of praise to the God of my life?

****

Memory sharpens in our crisis times and one sleepless night I recalled Mrs Green's words to us older girls after the death of her only son in the second world war: 'When tragedies like this come to us it's a great blessing to know God so intimately, and to trust him so completely that you don't need a special word or outward sign of God's presence. I've found it hard to be courageous and strong but, girls, it helps so much to know that God is there.'

The sincerity in her voice outweighed the sorrow in her eyes. As I listened I longed for faith like that, for trust so complete, even in such a devastating loss. I did not know then that God does not give us grace and strength for trials that we are not facing. He gives them when we need them.

And I needed them now, even as I remembered all that Mrs Green had shared with her Crusader girls.

God's words to the Old Testament hero Joshua came into my mind with new force, challenge and poignancy and refused to go away: 'Be strong and courageous. Do not be terrified; do not be discouraged, for the LORD your God will be with you wherever you go.'

God knew that I did not possess Mrs Green's spiritual calibre for coping with bereavement so in my distress he gave me a special word and a promise of his abiding presence. We often sang a chorus at Crusaders about being strong and very courageous, and the tune ran through my mind continuously on the way to Geoffrey's funeral, while the words remained for many days after. Their strengthening and sustaining power amaze me when I look back on that time so darkened by the shadow of death.

Reading took me out of myself and provided much comfort. I read *The Christian's Secret of a Happy Life* right through and often turned to my Bible. One day I read the first chapter of Revelation and became riveted to the words: 'I, John, who also am your brother, and companion in tribulation ... was in the isle that is called Patmos ... I was in the spirit on the Lord's day ... and I saw one like unto the Son of man ...'.

I closed my Bible and let the full impact of those words wash over me. Where was John, the disciple whom Jesus loved, when he had that glorious vision of his Saviour and Redeemer? On some exotic Hawaiian island with golden sands fringed by waving palms? No, but in exile - a Christian veteran banished by the emperor Domitian to a small, rock-strewn island of mines and quarries in the Aegean Sea.

During this time of suffering, abandonment and friendlessness, Christ revealed himself in a glorious new way. I meditated upon this and saw that there is still many a Patmos to be found along life's journey. They are stark, grey and forbidding islands, and yet they can prove to be the places where God's presence and upholding power are most strongly felt. One can even be 'in the Spirit' there!

In the solitude of my own Patmos Isle I knew that God understood my grief and heart-loneliness and he continued to whisper: 'Don't be afraid ... don't be dismayed ... I will be with you ...'.

I do not mean to imply that when I read about John on his barren island that I immediately overcame all grief.

Far from it. Despite God's whispered assurance, I still stumbled and groped my way through a fog of bewilderment. Some days I felt so emotionally drained and physically weak that I wondered how I would survive, how I would cope with tomorrow, and next week.

As for Christmas, daily drawing nearer, I dared not even think about it. My mother kept telling me that we should go away for the festive season, but I hated the idea and turned down one suggestion after another.

****

Two days before Christmas I slipped into a small country church where several children were putting the finishing touches to their Nativity project.

Instead of the traditional nativity scene with a straw-filled crib and animals standing round the Baby Jesus, these children had depicted the three Wise Men who came to Bethlehem with gifts for the infant Jesus. They had made a small house with a mud and straw roof. In the doorway sat a plastic doll dressed in blue Eastern robes. It represented Mary, and she had a smaller doll, as the young Jesus, on her lap.

Two richly dressed dolls, representing wise men from the east, stood before Mary with their gifts (one a chocolate wrapped in gold paper), and a little girl was trying to make a third doll kneel down. When she had succeeded she turned to me and said: 'That wise man is mine, and he's going back from Bethlehem by a different way.'

'All the wise men went home by a different road,' her

95

friend added. 'Our Sunday School teacher told us it was so that they didn't betray Jesus to the wicked king, Herod.'

A different way! Those words pierced me like darts. I had come to Christmas sad of heart and unwilling to join in any festivities. I kept telling God that I had accepted Geoffrey's death as something that he, in his wisdom, had allowed, but how I missed him!

Now Christmas had almost come, the time when we should draw near to Bethlehem, but my heart remained closed to the joy that the Christ Child came to bring. I had erected a wall of self-pity, firmly cemented into place by depression. That wall threatened to shut out God and man alike.

Suddenly, standing in that tiny country church, I felt ashamed of my reluctance to even go away that Christmas. My mother had insisted that a change would do both of us good, and she was right. Otherwise we would have had a lonely time, just the two of us, with me not exactly radiating Christmas cheer and goodwill.

Eventually I had yielded to her persuasion and we had joined a jolly, festive house party in a stately old house in the heart of the country. But my heart remained cold, devoid of goodwill, and I felt an alien amidst the laughter, the warm fellowship and general spirit of Christmas cheer. The other guests sang carols with gusto, but the joyous words stuck in my throat. God's message of peace remained unsung by me, the notes frozen before they could pass my lips.

As the hours dragged slowly by I found it harder and

harder to enter into the spirit of that house party. When I could no longer stand the strain I had crept away on my own. Grief made me an exile as I wandered along a winding, frost-covered path through a pinewood. I had become a soul apart, a martyr to deep inner pain.

My footsteps took me to a village with its grey stone church standing beside the green. When I slipped inside I had no idea that God awaited me. Certainly it never occurred to me that he would speak through the lips of a small girl: 'That wise man is mine, and he's going back a different way.'

In an instant I knew that I had to leave that church a changed person. In that shattering moment I left the children and sat in a nearby pew to think and pray. While I tried to collect my thoughts and calm my battered emotions, I gazed at the exquisite stained glass window above the altar. Then a shaft of winter sunshine shone through another window right beside me, showing up the brightly clad figures in the window's design. It reminded me of the child who said that a Christian is a person whom the light shines through. How dim my light had become!

The wall round my heart crumbled as I fell on my knees to ask God to pardon my dullness and gloom during the weeks before Christmas while I grappled with emotional turmoil. True, hope and courage had occasionally surfaced, but at other times my attitudes had been wholly negative. Now, as I prayed, God's peace and forgiveness flooded into my being, deep and abiding, like the calm below the wild raging of the ocean surface. And I knew that if, with God's help, I would direct my thoughts into more positive channels, then the glow would come back into my life.

I left the church and saw the little girls who had spoken to me chasing one another across the frosty green.

'Happy Christmas!' one of them shouted.

'Happy Christmas to you too,' I called back.

As the sunlight of God's peace continued to chase the dark shadows from my heart, I saw that to return in the same rut of self-pity would have been to betray the Christ Child, who came to show us a better way through life - a positive way of faith, hope and love.

In my eagerness to rejoin the house party, I forsook the winding woodland path in favour of a more direct route. I even found myself humming *O Little Town of Bethlehem* as I hurried along, lighter of step than I had been for many weeks.

Thankfulness to God welled up inside me that he had used a young child to tell me to go back into life by another way.

At the start of the new year, it finally dawned on me that, just as the sun shines only one day at a time, so God promises only enough strength for one day at a time. If I continued to allow his peace to enfold me and the sunshine of his love to chase fears and doubts away, then the year ahead would not be as dark and forbidding as I feared.

I had no marvellous vision such as bowed John down in awe and wonder on Patmos, but a deep inner assurance that God *would* strengthen, *would* sustain, *would* provide remained.

Chapter Ten

About a year after Geoffrey died the church youth club leaders arranged a house party at Greenhills, Worthing. Mrs Hitchcock, our minister's wife, tried to persuade me to go. I excused myself on the grounds that I was not in the right age group, nor did I feel equal to a weekend in the company of high-spirited teenagers. Undeterred, Mrs Hitchcock insisted that a change would do me good. So I went.

On the Saturday morning Douglas Wood, our minister's cousin, joined us. I had met him eighteen months previously at a similar house party, but Geoffrey had been with me then. Because he was an accountant, the young people had invited Geoffrey to be House Party Treasurer. We and Douglas had been the only three in our thirties. We also shared the same surname.

Now, Douglas had come over from Brighton again and we reintroduced ourselves. That afternoon Douglas suggested a walk and we went on the pier together to watch some anglers.

'Look, that one's caught a tadpole!' Douglas exclaimed.

We laughed as we watched the man winding in a small piece of bladderwrack seaweed, and felt easy in each other's company.

We walked and talked until rain drove us back to

Greenhills. There our conversation continued on a more serious level. I cannot recall how it came about, but we became deeply engrossed in the subject of predestination. This suited Douglas, who had graduated from a Bible College, but I soon felt out of my depth.

Steering the conversation into other channels, I discovered that Douglas had weathered many ups and downs, set-backs and reversals. Listening to him brought it home to me that widows do not have a monopoly of loneliness. Bachelors have their share as the years pass, and Douglas hinted that he had all but given up hope of meeting the one woman who would give him her love, understanding and companionship.

Douglas also confided that he had not wanted to come to Worthing that weekend but was glad he had yielded to his cousin's persuasion. Before we parted we both knew that a firm link had been forged in friendship's chain.

A few months later it pleased me that Douglas left Brighton to live temporarily at the manse, although I regretted the reason for this change. Through the scheming of a senior staff member where he worked, Douglas had been given notice. Today such a devious and underhand episode would be illegal, but the firm got away with it then.

'When I told my landlady that I'd lost my job, she promptly turned me out of my bed-sit,' Douglas added, with a wry smile.

'You must have done something wrong, or you wouldn't have been given notice,' she had maintained with pursed lips.

Douglas tried to explain that he had been pushed out to make way for a nephew of the senior man (Douglas later learned that this nephew walked out after a month), but his landlady relented only slightly. She insisted that Douglas must leave her house by the end of the year.

'I spent the next few weeks job and lodging hunting, but without success,' Douglas continued, 'so I arrived at the manse jobless and homeless.'

'That's tough,' I sympathized.

'But I believe the Lord will show me in his own time what I'm to do, and where,' Douglas added confidently.

He spoke without bitterness or rebellion, even without anxiety, which won my admiration. He was concerned to do the right thing, yes, but not anxious.

Faith's reward came when Douglas obtained a post in an international telephone exchange. He settled down happily and discovered that he had better prospects than his previous job could have offered, and he later became a supervisor. Douglas also found an ideal bed-sitter near my home with a more considerate landlady.

One evening we walked home together from our friend Norrie's house. A bitter north-east wind chilled us and I was grateful to Douglas for his kindness in lending me his fur-lined gloves, while he trudged along with his hands in his pockets. I had left my own gloves at church earlier in the evening.

I appreciated many such kindnesses from Douglas. Little things that typified his thoughtful nature. Our friendship deepened and the warmth of it did wonders in healing my broken heart. Douglas had lost his mother, who died in Ireland, while he stayed at the manse, and he passed on to me much of the comfort with which God comforted him. Mutual sorrow drew us even closer to each other.

Another snowy Sunday evening a young couple, Jenny and Mike, gave us a lift home after church. They dropped me first, then Jenny said to Douglas: 'I don't know how Christine stands living alone like that. Isn't she plucky?'

Douglas later told me that he smiled to himself when Jenny said that because he intended to end my loneliness. He became a frequent and welcome visitor to my home. The more I got to know him the more I liked him. And that liking grew until I fell in love with him.

'I've loved you for months but kept it to myself because I felt it was too soon to tell you,' Douglas said, after we had revealed our feelings for each other.

That was typical of Douglas, thoughtful, considerate and patient. The next time he came to see me he insisted that we went shopping. 'Whatever for?' I asked.

'Well, I've just received an income tax refund for my weeks of unemployment. We're spending it on an engagement ring,' he explained, a warm, tender smile crinkling the corners of his deep blue eyes.

'May I have a ring with a ruby in it?' I asked. 'You see, I'd like the ring to remind me of the woman in the last chapter of Proverbs.'

'You choose what you like,' Douglas agreed, so we set off on our quest for a ruby engagement ring.

We found exactly what I wanted in the first jewellers

we tried. In all the excitement we both fancied a cup of tea, so we went on to the restaurant in a nearby department store. There Douglas slipped the ring on my finger.

'On top of many other good things, God is giving me a wife,' Douglas smiled, and we both knew that the sun that had set on so much distress for both of us was moving towards a bright tomorrow.

****

Because of my long association with the Exclusive Brethren, Geoffrey and I had married in a Registry Office. This time Douglas and I enjoyed a church wedding. His cousin, the Rev WJH Hitchcock, married us and it warmed my heart the way many friends and well-wishers surrounded us with their love. The young people at the church, most of whom had known Geoffrey, especially took a lively interest and turned up in force to enjoy our special day.

Even my mother came to the marriage service, although she took no interest in the wedding arrangements, and I welcomed her slight change of attitude.

Our good friend Norrie agreed to be an usher while his wife Jeanna capably undertook responsibility for our homely reception in the church hall. Dick and Ruby, two other friends who ran a restaurant, made our wedding cake (refusing payment) and many of the young people either waited at the tables or worked hard in the kitchen. So much warmth and goodwill left us almost lost for words.

We spent our honeymoon in Weston-Super-Mare. We had just six short days because we wanted to be back for the wedding of our pastor's eldest son, whose fiancée had been my bridesmaid the previous Saturday. But we made the most of those six days, walking and shouting above the bracing winds and getting to know each other ever more intimately.

On our return home cards and letters of goodwill still lay scattered on the table and sideboard, along with many presents. I paused in my tidying up to look through the letters and cards again. Everything had been so rushed before the wedding that I had not fully appreciated them. It would have been heartless to put them away in a box without savouring afresh the kindness of the many dear friends who had showered Douglas and me with their good wishes.

Among the letters lay a special one from Win, a long-standing friend. As I picked up her letter I could see Win in my mind's eye - plump, motherly, and forthright. Win had been among the first to write and as I reread her letter I appreciated afresh her caring wisdom:

'This has been a terrible time for you,' she wrote, 'and you deserve some happiness. I'm quite sure Geoffrey would be happy too, and would feel you are doing the right thing. Now I hope all goes well, and a new life will open up for you, containing a happiness such as you knew with Geoffrey.

But take a word of warning - the moment you begin to find yourself comparing your new husband, or his ways, with things as they were with Geoffrey, then start thinking about something else right away. Get up and do some other job, anything to stop yourself thinking this way! If you don't, when you find he is different, as he will be, then will be the time when troubles are likely to crop up. I understand Douglas is a bachelor so he has no previous experience to call on. This means that all the adjustment will be on your side. He doesn't as yet know what it's like to live a married life, and you have to teach him!! Give and take, as we married folk know from experience ...'.

Before Win's letter came I had been deeply conscious that by remarrying I would be walking on an entirely new stretch of road. How could I expect it to be the same when God never takes us over the same span of time twice? He always has something different to guide us into, with new experiences, and different horizons to beckon us on.

'How can you be sure that it will be the same when you remarry?' my anxious and well-meaning friend Rosemary asked when Douglas and I became engaged. I had tried to explain that I did not expect this new relationship to be a carbon copy of the first, but she could only shake her head in doubtful uncertainty. Now, here was Win's letter, so typical of her down-to-earth approach to life. She understood, and her letter strengthened me.

Yet, even as I folded Win's letter, I could not help thinking in how many small ways Douglas and Geoffrey *were* alike. True, their physiques were entirely different.

Geoffrey was sturdily built with broad shoulders, whereas Douglas was tall and slim, almost too thin. When we became engaged I resolved to fatten him up. I would give him good, solid meals in place of the snacks he cooked in his bed-sit. (After I had gained two stone and Douglas remained the same weight, I gave up on this attempt.)

But what Douglas lacked in physique he more than made up for in strength of character. Like Geoffrey, he stood for justice and fair play, a man of integrity. In the Bible it says of Paul's friend Barnabas that he was 'a good man'. That brief description summed up Douglas too, and I thanked God for the two good men in my life.

I replaced Win's letter in its envelope and as I sorted letters and cards into two separate piles, I thought of other surprising similarities in two such different men. Because of his early training in his father's dental practice, Geoffrey had a most methodical way of dealing with tools. Whenever he broke off from a job he would line his tools up in a neat row, just as a dentist lays out his instruments on a dental tray. It astonished me to find that Douglas, who knew nothing of this, did exactly the same thing.

Endearing similarities among so many differences. I pulled myself up with a jerk. Was I about to make the very comparisons that Win had warned against?

Tidying up requires little concentration so while I continued sorting letters from cards I deliberately redirected my thoughts to the chain of events that had brought Win into my life.

Writing had become my hobby while Geoffrey studied. Although it satisfied me to see stories and articles in print, writing proved a lonely occupation. Sometimes I found it more companionable to read books that someone else had written.

We lived near the local library and one evening I strolled over to change some books. An advertisement on the notice-board attracted my attention. It read: THE WRITERS' CIRCLE invites you to its literary evenings ... stories read ... manuscripts discussed ... suitable markets suggested.

It delighted me to discover that other writers lived in the neighbourhood, and I hurried home to tell Geoffrey this exciting news. He encouraged me to join the Circle, so I found myself among novelists, playwrights and film scriptwriters.

At first all this professionalism daunted me and I felt very much the new girl, yet it would have been hard to find a friendlier group. The only intimidating member was a rough diamond who wrote Wild Westerns and barked out his criticisms of other people's work like military orders.

I look back with gratitude on the friendliness of the playwrights Leone Stuart and Aileen Burke. Their cheerful encouragement gave my morale a boost. Then there was the charming, warm-hearted novelist Dianne Doubtfire who urged me to 'think big and aim high'.

Aileen Burke breezed into one circle meeting full of her usual cheerful enthusiasm.

'Who's coming to Swanwick?' she beamed. 'How about you, Christine? Do come to Swanwick!'

'Where and what is it?' I asked.

'It's the Writers' Summer School in Derbyshire,' her sister Leone explained.

Aileen handed me an application form and urged

immediate application as applications always exceeded places at the school. 'Swanwick can only accommodate three hundred,' she said.

Three hundred! The thought of mixing with so many writers alarmed me but Geoffrey overruled my reservations by filling in the application form and posting it off before I could change my mind.

I gained a place at the School and later arrived at what I think of as Scribblers' Haven - a beautiful, self-contained entity comprising a gracious old grey stone house surrounded by vegetable gardens, lawns, meadowland, magnificent trees, a farm and last but not least, a duck pond where I retreated when I felt the need to 'get away from it all' for a while.

But what a stimulating experience that School proved to be! I would not have missed it for anything. One of the first writers to whom I felt drawn was a sweet-faced little lady several years my senior who walked with a crutch. Elsie told me that she wrote and illustrated her own children's stories, and a mutual interest in writing for children linked us in friendship.

'This is my first time at the school and I feel rather strange and inadequate,' Elsie confided and I empathized with that too.

We shared confidences and ambitions and after the School we teamed up on work for *The Christian Herald*. I wrote stories for the children's page which Elsie turned into serialised picture strips.

While at Swanwick Elsie told me that she illustrated

Brownie stories for Win, who also attended the School that year. She introduced us and I liked the way strong, motherly Win allowed frail, little Elsie to lean on her arm to avoid slipping on the shiny floors. And so a long-standing friendship with Win began that year as well.

While still day-dreaming about Elsie and Win, I searched for a box in which to keep the wedding cards and letters. Swanwick endeared itself to me over the years and I still look forward to my annual reunion with the friends I have made there. Elsie, alas, is no longer one of them but I like to recall how several of us, Win and Elsie included, formed into a happy fellowship that gathered round a log fire at the end of each day to share our writing experiences and problems while enjoying the warmth of the flickering flames.

'Time brings changes,' I mused, as I found the box I wanted.

Elsie's disabilities soon prevented her from attending the Summer School and other commitments kept Win away but, as I put her letter in the box, I knew I would always cherish memories of that big, open fire and the warm glow reflected on each friendly face –Win's per-haps the dearest among them.

I put the box in a cupboard but the wise guidance that she had given me over my second marriage I tucked away in my heart. As I did so, I felt I owed that writers' haven a lot for bringing a friend like Win into my life.

Chapter Eleven

As my friend Win had warned me, I found life with Douglas different, yet with a sameness about the difference. That sounds contradictory, but in everyday happenings I discovered that our happiness revolved round alternative versions of the same things. Among them were amusing incidents that we could laugh over.

Geoffrey had been a keen cyclist and shortly after we married he bought a second-hand tandem. We rode through miles of Surrey countryside on this old tandem. Late one summer evening we rounded a bend and nearly mowed down what I can only describe as a public rabbit rally.

Dozens of rabbits covered the road and looked as if they were listening to a political talk from a large, dark-haired rabbit sitting up on its hind legs, ears erect and alert. Our speedy approach disturbed this public meeting and rows of rabbits scattered in all directions. We braked so sharply that we fell off the tandem. We did not hurt ourselves but sat beside the road helpless with laughter.

Douglas and I laughed in the same way during a weekend in Cambridge, where loud quacking in the botanical gardens drew us towards the duck pond. There we found anxious ducks trying to guide and protect their ducklings in an overcrowded swimming space. All round the harassed mothers other ducks fought and squabbled.

We had no idea what sparked off so much commotion but stood on the bank to watch the armada-type scene of flaying wings and pecking beaks. Feathers flew as quacking reached an ear-splitting crescendo.

Suddenly a big-boss duck led the whole contingent, apart from the mothers with ducklings, out of the water. The ducks arranged themselves in rows to an undertone of low quacks while ruffled feathers were smoothed.

The big-boss duck took his place at the front, his breast swollen with importance as he faced the ranks. He launched into an impassioned speech, delivered in a series of loud, dictatorial quacks.

The audience listened in respectful silence, except for a dissenter in the back row who heckled in noisy quacks. His speech over, the big-boss duck joined the ranks and the opposing duck waddled forward to express his views in a few staccato quacks. His remarks were brief and to the point and the meeting soon ended. Order was restored and the ducks filed quietly back to the water.

Douglas and I could not contain our laughter and sat on a nearby seat with tears streaming down our faces. Even as I recall this amusing scene it reminds me that, on the human level, much of our happiness is made up of little incidents shared with those we love. Different, yes, but with a delightful sameness.

Douglas also shared my interest in writing and accompanied me to two Christian Writing Schools organized by the Billy Graham Organization. We also joined the Fellowship of Christian Writers, which partly had its roots in one of these schools.

Dr. Sherwood Wirt, who was then editor of *Decision* magazine, came over from Minneapolis to teach at these schools (as well as to assist with Billy Graham Crusades being held prior to the schools). In conversation with Dr. Wirt I inadvertently mentioned that I had written several children's books. I say inadvertently because Dr. Wirt immediately asked me to give a talk on writing for children.

This request sent me into a 'panic attack' with its attendant internal disorder, a problem with which I had battled for years. This irrational fear of public speaking was a hangover from my Exclusive Brethren days. Geoffrey, with gentle understanding and encouragement, had helped me to overcome it, but with only partial success.

This fear robbed me of much that I would have enjoyed doing, such as joining the church Wives Fellowship. I refused to do so, much as I longed to join, because I knew the wives took it in turn to run informal Bible Studies within the group. The very idea terrified me.

I had twice spent an evening with this group when the leader had specifically invited me to talk to them. I had agreed with great reluctance and on both occasions an acute attack of 'nervous colitis' had laid me low for several days. Only Geoffrey knew what it cost me to give those talks.

Had I confided my problem to the leader I am sure she

would have shown sympathetic understanding, but embarrassment and pride prevented me. Geoffrey encouraged me to give these talks because he thought I would best overcome fear by doing what I feared most. Good psychology perhaps, but hard to put into practice.

Now, here was Dr. Wirt asking me to address a classroom of students. My heart raced and palms sweated, but I agreed to do it. Illness struck beforehand but the bottle of Mist. Kaolin et Morph. in my suitcase helped calm the distressing symptoms as I hastily prepared the talk. I persisted because I really wanted to give that talk. Even more, I longed to overcome this fear phantom that so often gagged me.

The students took a lively interest in that talk and many expressed a keenness to try writing for children. My nervousness vanished as I answered their many and varied questions.

After this session I saw Dr. Wirt sitting beside a fountain in the garden so I went over to tell him how my session had gone. I did not have to report in this way, but did it on a sudden impulse. Just a small, casual action.

June, a friend of mine, becomes annoyed if I refer to any happening as 'only a small thing'.

'Christine, there are no small things in the Christian life,' she asserts. 'Every little thing is part of some bigger thing.'

June's theory proved correct in this instance because, as I joined Dr. Wirt beside that fountain, I had no idea how far-reaching the result would be. We had chatted a while when Dr. Wirt astounded me with another request.

'We're publishing a British edition of *Decision* next year and I'd like you to be our British Editorial Associate. Will you take on this work?' he asked.

'But I know nothing about editing,' I protested.

'You'll learn as you go along,' Dr. Wirt assured me.

'Actually I've just given up work to concentrate more on my writing,' I further objected.

'Ah, you followed the Lord's leading by quitting your job. Now he's showing you the next step,' Dr. Wirt smiled confidently.

How does one resist a man like that? I could only play for time and said I would have to think and pray about it before taking on such a responsibility. Dr. Wirt agreed to wait and I promised to write to him with my decision.

Douglas surprised me by his enthusiasm when I told him of this unexpected request.

'Give it a try,' he advised. 'You'll be working at home so won't even waste time travelling.'

After much prayerful consideration, I agreed to attempt this editorial work and Dr. Wirt expressed his pleasure at my willingness. The challenge excited me and I hoped Dr. Wirt would not be disappointed in his choice of associate.

It proved a difficult transition from writing children's books to editing and criticising adult inspirational and devotional articles.

'I'd feel happier if I could write this kind of thing myself,' I told Douglas. 'I don't like pointing out defects in other people's work when I can't do it myself.'

'Well, there's a simple remedy. Write something,' Douglas said, practical as ever.

I discovered it was much easier to read other writers' manuscripts than to prepare one myself. It embarrassed me to bare my soul in a 'personal experience' story, as required by *Decision*. I made several abortive attempts and nearly gave up because my efforts sounded either trite or sermonizing.

Did I have the right kind of spiritual experience to share anyway? I could not just relate happenings for their own sake. They needed to be encounters with God that opened the door to an ongoing spiritual process. I should aim at encouraging readers to a deeper personal commitment to God but found it a daunting, heart-searching aim. Who was I to offer encouragement of this kind?

But I went on trying. I also edited with a new respect the articles that other writers submitted to me.

****

Brrrrr......... Brrrrr......... Brrrrr.........

I hurried to the telephone. If yet another caller wanted the garage on the main road I would ask Douglas to complain to the Telephone Exchange about these misdirected calls.

'Hello, yes? This is ...'.

'Sure sounds like you, Christine. Can I come down for a coffee with you?'

'Dr. Wirt! Come right away, I didn't even know you were back in England.'

I gave directions from London and hung up.

I had been British Editorial Associate for *Decision* for over a year and received a lot of support and encouragement from Sherwood Wirt and his staff in Minneapolis. It would be great to see him again.

Dr. Wirt's photographer accompanied him. He took several shots of me sitting at my typewriter, one of which would be used to illustrate an article I had submitted to *Decision*. Yes, I finally made it and had an article accepted!

Before they left, I showed Dr. Wirt and the photographer round my home and said that if ever either of them passed this way again, they would be welcome to spend a night or two in the small guest room.

'Ah, your prophet's chamber!' Dr. Wirt exclaimed, alluding to the article he had accepted.

I partly overcame my struggle with 'personal experience' stories by writing an article on several Bible characters who believed in a Do-it-Yourself approach to life. The opening of a Do-it-Yourself shop in our neighbourhood had sparked off the idea. After buying supplies at this shop, Douglas had made a wardrobe for our 'prophet's chamber', as Dr. Wirt had called it.

While I helped Douglas my thoughts had circled round the do-it yourself concept. Was this idea so modern? Hadn't creativity always been around? After all, the first pages of Genesis devote themselves to relating all that

God made, culminating with God saying: 'Let us make man in our image' - the image of a creative God.

The article had taken shape as I thought of various people in the Bible who had said: 'Let us make ...'. Sometimes, I found, creativity had been put to a bad use, like the golden calf that Israelite rebels made to worship in Moses' day. Even before that, rebellious Babylonian builders had tried to make a name for themselves by building a tower that reached to the skies.

On the positive side, I recalled several other do-it-yourselfers who put creativity to a good use, like the Shunammite woman who said to her husband: 'Let us make a little room for the prophet Elisha to stay in when he is passing this way'–a suggestion that had far-reaching results.

I enjoyed writing that *Decision* article but left myself out of it as far as possible. Only towards the end did I confess that when I try the 'do-it-yourself approach' I often make a mess of things. I become disappointed and discouraged, and then my husband says: 'Why didn't you wait for me to show you how?'

God often has to say that to me too, as I admitted in the article. Douglas acquired his do-it-yourself knowledge by reading practical magazines. God has also shown me 'how' in his book, the Bible, but I need to take time to study it. I shared with *Decision* readers the good news that God not only shows us 'how' when we are willing to learn but, when we do not crowd him out by self-effort, he also empowers us to do his work.

When the article appeared in *Decision*, I wondered if I had 'arrived' when it came to writing inspirational articles. In fact I still had much to learn. As Dr. Wirt had predicted, I learned a lot of it through editing other writers' work and devising better ways of saying the same thing.

But I never gave a thought to where the experience gained might lead me. Such possible future activities as teaching large classes of students how to write never entered my head. Although I gave that hastily prepared talk on children's books, I hardly ranked as an expert. But then, as my friend June says, every small thing in the Christian life is part of some bigger thing. It is just that God does not reveal the whole picture at once.

Decision work occupied only part of my time. After a while the ambitious, restive side of my nature longed to do something more productive for God. My publishers compounded the problem by writing to say that, owing to a change of policy, they no longer required children's books. Disappointment added to the frustration.

During this unsettled time Dorothy, a long-standing friend, gave me a cutting from her deep-pink African violet. The cutting flourished and became a thick mass of leaves, but the plant bore only a few sickly flowers on stunted stems. Perplexed, I turned to Dorothy for advice.

'The pot's too big,' she explained. 'You've allowed the plant to spread and become weakened by overgrowth. These violets bloom best in a small pot.'

As I looked at my leafy, overgrown plant, my own

circumstances suddenly appeared less confining. Although I dreamed of a bigger place in which to spread my roots and to enjoy a wider sphere of Christian service, God in his wisdom knew best. I came to see that he chooses some to bear fruit in a large area of activity and equips them accordingly. But others, like myself, flourish best when confined to a small place where we cannot spread our resources too thinly or too widely. That way we can blossom into full achievement with no waste of spiritual energy or strength.

My work might not appear important or impressive, but I understood that I would bloom effectively if I remained content to fulfil the role that God intended. I wasn't a very apt pupil, but I was also beginning to appreciate the value of that little word WAIT.

Chapter Twelve

I had to keep reminding myself of the lesson that Dorothy's African violet had taught me. It helped me not to fret now that my publishers no longer required children's books.

But when would God show me what to do next? Wasn't there some more fulfilling enterprise than running a maisonette, shopping and part-time editorial work? The African violet ceased blooming, but I threw myself into a frenzy of activity: cleaning, decorating and gardening. I also made several trips to London to choose books for the church bookstall I ran, struggling home laden with heavy parcels.

My hang-up over public speaking still haunted me but I refused to admit defeat and gave talks at meetings of the Fellowship of Christian Writers. These opportunities proved the breakthrough in overcoming panic attacks. Grateful as I was for this breakthrough, I still had impatience and other flaws in my character to face up to.

Overwork and inner unrest took their toll and once again my health suffered. I reacted with rebellion, especially as we were about to go on holiday.

'What's the use of going if this illness is going to persist?' I complained to Douglas.

'Of course we're going. You need a holiday,' he replied, and calmly packed his case.

I arrived at the holiday flat tired and dispirited but

rallied at the beautiful sea view from the windows. The next day I seethed with impatience when Douglas went exploring. I longed to go with him but instead I rested on the balcony and watched the scudding white clouds.

Slowly I came to terms with this enforced inactivity and even uttered a prayer similar to Jacob's at Peniel: 'Lord, please don't let this illness go until it has blessed me.' That cry was wrung from my heart.

I had no clear idea how sickness could be a blessing, but then God often surprises us by answering our prayers in unexpected ways. He used an old autograph album to get through to me with that particular blessing.

I had found the album a few weeks previously while tidying our loft. At the time I had merely flicked through the pages, but I had brought the album away to look at properly. In it I read: 'Patience is a virtue; possess it if you can. It is sometimes found in women, seldom in a man.' A school friend had written this little exhortation in big, rounded handwriting and now God used it to direct my thoughts.

Although so often challenged, what did I really know of this once-prized virtue? Not much. But then, I reasoned, the twentieth century is not exactly geared to patience. This fruit of the Spirit which Paul listed in his letter to the Galatians has a hard time to survive in this press-button age of ever-increasing speed. Once again God tried to get through to me, but excuses leaped to my defence because I didn't want to face up to the fact that many of the mistakes in my life had impatience at their roots.

My mind flicked back to the kitchen cupboard I was about to clean when illness struck. It contained instant mashed potatoes, instant cake mixes, instant coffee ... then the postman had brought Douglas a credit card offer which guaranteed to 'take the wait out of wanting'. With everything geared to a 'now' that rushes into the past if one doesn't grab it, how could I be patient?

God gently pushed aside all these reasonings and excuses. His blessing had to involve my listening, learning and then being willing to change my whirlwind lifestyle.

At last I admitted that my life, both spiritually and physically, had long been marred by impatience. As I dashed off to the shops or to visit a sick friend or rushed to a speaking engagement, I considered myself a useful, mature Christian. But God saw things differently.

He confronted me with the uncomfortable truth that, instead of waiting upon his timing, I was a victim of the rat race. In this sobering moment I saw that to abuse my body by rush and overwork could never be God-honouring. It took that painful bout of colitis to get me still enough and quiet enough to hear the whisper of God's voice.

Nature also enacted a parable to reinforce the message. Each day I sat on the balcony to watch the tide flowing over golden sand. Patience gained a foothold in my life as I learned to wait for increased well-being. I also grew to love the therapeutic sight and sound of ebbing and flowing water.

'A penny for your day-dreams,' Douglas said one morning.

'I'm noticing how the tide comes in gradually, not in one great rat race of a rush,' I told him. 'Look, the waves thrust forward, retreat, and then another wave thrusts further forward after each recession.'

'That's not new. The tide's been doing that for a long time,' Douglas smiled.

'I know, but it appears such a negative moment when the water recedes, yet those negative moments pave the way for full advancement up the beach.'

'You're learning to meditate. No wonder you're more relaxed,' Douglas said. No criticism. Just kindness.

As I watched this daily parable unfold, I reflected that my illness had also appeared a negative, regressive thing. Yet it too could pave the way to greater progress in Christian work and the spiritual maturity for which I longed if I applied to it all that the tide was teaching me. This drawing back time could, like the ebbing water, give greater impetus to a future thrust forward provided I accepted it positively, instead of fretting.

That holiday proved to be a special time after all. God answered my prayer for a blessing by showing me that in order to function effectively, I first needed to acquire that all-important grace of patience. I thought I had got the message at last and soon became well enough to enjoy more active days. It did not occur to me then that there would still be future lapses to deal with.

As I strolled along the seashore, the lapping of the water continued to be a balm to my restless spirit. God also spoke to me in the whisper of the summer breeze and the gentle swish of the calm, tranquil sea.

His message, and his blessing, did not end there though. He still had much more to say to me on that holiday, and he used a small stone to say it.

I saw the stone rolling down the beach in the shallow water, and scooped it up before the ebbing tide could carry it beyond my grasp. Lapidary had become my husband's latest craze, and he promised to polish any stone that took my fancy. I certainly fancied this little pear-shaped one, and when it lay in the palm of my hand, it looked even more attractive.

Douglas examined the stone with care.

'It has a slight irregularity of shape and a rough surface, but no flaw that my tumble-polisher won't put right,' he assured me. He also said it would make a charming pendant, so I looked forward to seeing the finished product of his latest skill.

We returned home much refreshed by our holiday and Douglas put the opaque stone in his tumbler, along with several others. There they jostled and rubbed against each other while the tumble-polisher rotated slowly for three whole weeks. If stones could feel, it would have been an uncomfortable experience, but it resulted in a thing of beauty.

When Douglas showed me my special stone I was delighted. The slight irregularity of shape had gone, leaving the stone smooth and shining, its opacity enhanced. 'It's lovely!' I exclaimed. 'Aren't you clever to make something so attractive out of an ordinary pebble from the seashore!'

'It's not just ordinary,' he protested. 'It's special because you chose it.'

Some half-remembered verses from Peter's first letter teased my mind about God choosing certain people to declare his wonderful deeds. Jesus was also referred to as the chosen Cornerstone whose followers would not be put to shame. I scoured my memory. What exactly did that passage say about stones? I found the place in my Bible and read: 'Come to him, to that living stone, rejected by men but in God's sight chosen and precious; and like living stones be yourselves built into a spiritual house ... that you may declare the wonderful deeds of him who called you out of darkness into his marvellous light.'

Before I could share these words with Douglas, he said something which I shall surely always remember: 'The art of lapidary is knowing exactly how much friction a stone needs to make it shine.'

His words riveted my attention as I gazed at my treasure. I, too, was a stone, a living stone in God's spiritual house, and he knew exactly how much friction I needed to make me shine for him.

In that moment of enlightenment the frustrations and other burdens that had weighed me down assumed their proper proportions. Sometimes I considered that I had had more than my share of problems and disappointments, but now I knew I had not. I had to bear only what God in his wisdom allowed.

God also showed me that, because I was a stone in his spiritual house, he had been shaping me into the finished product that he wanted me to be. He had a place for me and a plan that I should fit into, but I would not fit until he had smoothed away the jagged edges in my make-up. Impatience continually needed dealing with, but the list of my shortcomings grew even as I meditated: wrong attitudes, mixed motives, an unruly tongue, these and other imperfections and rough corners would have to be smoothed away before I would fit into God's spiritual house.

In his wisdom, God had allowed disappointments, closed doors and other trials to do their refining work. And he was doing it, not to make me unhappy, but to mould my character and lovingly fashion me into the person he wanted me to be–a living, shining stone that would declare his wonderful deeds.

Douglas finished working on the opaque, pear-shaped stone and presented it to me in the form of a dainty pendant on a chain, just as he had promised. That pendant is the work of a craftsman who took a great deal of care in its making. Whenever I wore it I knew it would be a valuable reminder that if Douglas could take so much care over a pebble from the beach, then how much greater is God's care. He knows how much of life's rough and tumble I need to shine for him, including accepting disappointments and learning to wait for his perfect timing.

I praise God still for the message of that little stone. It fills me with hope that one day I shall slot perfectly into place in his spiritual house.

Not only did I enjoy wearing that little stone, but it worked for me in unexpected ways, ending my waiting time. Its message so impressed itself upon my heart that I shared it with *Decision* readers, with surprising results.

Decision adds a brief biographical footnote to its articles, including which church the writer worships at. Several letters reached me via the church after publication of my stone story. One immediately aroused my curiosity. I turned over the cream envelope to find the red crest of the House of Lords on the flap. Intrigued, I opened it at once.

'Read it when we get home,' my husband whispered, as I pulled out a sheet of crested notepaper.

That instruction put too much strain on my slow-growing patience. After all, I did not receive letters from the nobility every day.

One of the peers had written to say how my article had restored his peace of mind after a time of particular stress and tension. A sense of awe filled my heart as I read that letter. Had God really used me to help someone so far above my station in life?

More followed. First an air letter from an American geologist who also lectured in universities. He requested permission to reprint the article.

'I would like to give a copy to all my geology students,' he wrote, and I gladly gave my consent.

A second, similar request came from another American, this time a professor training young men for the ministry. He wished to do the same for his students.

A third letter opened up undreamed of writing opportunities. It came about so quietly that I did not even know that my 'waiting time' had ended. I did not have to put my shoulder to the door, nor even push it. God used the writer of this letter to open the door, and I simply walked through into a new sphere of writing.

This man wrote from Texas to say that my article had so encouraged him when the going was hard that he would like to express his appreciation by sending me a gift. I did not see why he should send anything. The fact that the article had helped him was reward enough for writing it, so I put the letter aside without replying. About three weeks later this man wrote again asking what I would like. In the meantime a friend had told me how helpful she had found *The Successful Writers and Editors Guidebook*, which her husband had bought her while in the States.

'This book lists American Christian publishers, both of books and magazines,' my friend had told me. 'Since using it I've had several acceptances.'

Right. If Daphne could do it, so could I. So I wrote to my generous correspondent asking for a copy of this literary guide.

'It's on its way,' he airmailed back, and it later arrived by surface mail.

That guide transformed my writing life and I threw myself into writing devotional and inspirational articles for many American publications. This overcame my disappointment about children's books, and I felt happy and fulfilled in this new sphere.

Ripples! And all from one small stone.

Chapter Thirteen

Douglas and I regretted the day when his cousin left our church to take up a new pastorate in Norfolk. Sadder days followed when the church foundered without leadership for many months and eventually adopted an entirely different emphasis in worship.

These differences divided the youth club and many young people left, never to return. We did all we could to keep things on an even keel but one-time friends shouted us down and we, two of a small minority group, had to admit defeat.

It shook me to face this kind of trauma again. Hadn't I gone through enough when leaving the Exclusive Brethren? After a final, painful confrontation, Douglas and I knew in our hearts that we, too, had walked out of the church doors for the last time. The next day we went to a restaurant in a neighbouring town to 'get away from it all' and to come to terms with our sense of rejection. We ordered a meal but cried so much that we could not eat it. We left the table, conscious of curious glances from the diners around us.

After much heart-searching, we resigned membership and moved to another church renowned for its Bible-based, Christ-centred teaching. Although some distance from our home, this church stirred vague memories. Had

I not been here before? The years fell away as memory sharpened. Of course I had! Mrs Green used to attend this church and had taken me to two or three gospel outreach services when I was about sixteen.

Douglas and I received a warm welcome and we soon settled in our new spiritual home. A lady with greenish-grey eyes who I judged to be in her early seventies often smiled at me and I found something magnetic about that smile. This lady wore her greying hair in two plaits coiled round like headphones and I admired her firm jawline. Before we had even spoken to each other. somehow her strong personality came across. I learned that her name was Mrs Walton and she won sympathetic glances from me because she had to stand at the back of the church during sermons.

'Gladys Walton's plagued with back pain,' a new friend answered my enquiry.

I often suffered from backache myself, especially after typing for too long. Although not as serious as Mrs Walton's condition, my back pain made me care about her problem. An air cushion often eased my backache, so I bought one for Mrs Walton in the hope that it would help her too.

As I did not really know Gladys Walton, it embarrassed me to give her that cushion, but she quickly put me at ease. She thanked me in a strong Yorkshire accent which hinted at the vibrant character of the person who owned it.

Just a small thing (are there any?), but this simple

action led to friendship with a radiant Christian who influenced me as profoundly as Mrs Green had done in my youth.

Shortly after giving the cushion, Mrs Walton and I met in the street. She walked slowly with the aid of a stick, so I asked if her back had improved at all.

'Not much, but then I must expect aches and pains at my age,' Mrs Walton told me, cheerful and forthright.

I slowed my pace to match hers and walked along with her.

'I'm glad we met today because I've been praying for you,' Mrs Walton surprised me by saying. 'I run a Bible Study group in my home, just eight of us, but one lady has moved away. I've been asking the Lord about a replacement and you keep coming into my mind. I believe it's the Lord's prompting.'

Why me? We hardly knew each other. But I accepted the invitation and the other members of the group (mostly Anglicans) also accepted me. I grew to love those fortnightly studies, and basked in the warm, friendly atmosphere in Mrs Walton's drawing-room.

In Mrs Walton I found a friend to whom I knew I could turn if life became hard or problems weighed me down. She had a way of saying the right thing just when I needed it most. But she had paid a high price for her skilful sensitivity in treating hurts and drying tears, since it is not possible to help another person beyond your own experience.

Like Mrs Green so long ago, Mrs Walton knew much

about 'the furnace of affliction'. Instead of embittering her, it had moulded her into an understanding, sympathetic lady well equipped to help others.

Sometimes Mrs Walton invited me for a morning coffee, just the two of us, and I found those mornings real 'mountain top' experiences. Friendship deepened and we shared much of our past lives with each other.

Mrs Walton's husband had, like Geoffrey, died young, leaving her with two daughters to bring up. This mutual loss in our younger days did much to draw us together.

'How long have you been a Christian?' Mrs Walton asked me.

'Since I was twelve,' I told her. 'I was converted at Crusaders and owe a lot to Mrs Green who taught me during my teens. She was once a member of our church. Isn't it strange that I should become a member after all these years?'

'It's the right time for you, dear. God's timing is always perfect. We can safely trust him and go by his clock,' Mrs Walton beamed.

How wise I found her! Not like me, prone to either lag behind or rush ahead, instead of keeping in step with the Spirit, as the apostle Paul put it.

'Mrs Green, did you say?' Gladys Walton broke in on my thoughts. 'She once led the church Women's Meeting that I now lead.'

What a coincidence! I felt as if my life had turned full circle, and a warm glow flooded my being. God had blessed me with this dear friend who would love me as

Mrs Green had done. I loved her, too, and thought of her as my spiritual Mum.

In Mrs Walton I had found a true prayer warrior. Because of her example my own prayer life took on a new dimension. It deepened and widened under her influence as we united to bring God our worship, thanks and requests.

'God does nothing but in answer to prayer', wrote John Wesley and Mrs Walton certainly believed it. She showed me the privilege and responsibility of an effective prayer life.

'God chooses not to work independently but acts when we pray. Isn't that amazing grace?' she said.

I talked to God in a new, vital way in my private prayer times. I also listened to his voice while I meditated on his Word, and he blessed me with growth towards spiritual maturity and understanding. But I still had so far to go.

'You look tired. Have you been overtaxing yourself?' Mrs Walton asked during one of our coffee mornings.

I didn't pretend I hadn't because she would have seen through such pretence anyway, so I confessed my besetting sin.

'There's always so much to do,' I lamented, and Mrs Walton looked at me with serious grey-green eyes.

'You know, dear, I've always been glad Jesus didn't pray: "Father, I have finished the work",' she said. 'What did he pray?'

I hesitated and did some quick thinking.

'Wasn't it: "I have finished the work you gave me to do"?' I asked.

'That's right. None of us can ever finish all the work to be done. We need to know which work God has in mind for *us*,' Mrs Walton replied.

I appreciated her wisdom, but would I act upon it?

****

Amid all the unrest at our previous church, our good friends Norrie and Jeanna, together with their two children, emigrated to Canada. We lost contact for a while so it was with extra pleasure that I received an air letter from Jeanna.

'We've moved from Vancouver because the bank have put Norrie in charge of a branch in the Rockies,' she wrote. 'McBride is a small place with no made up roads, but we'd love to see you two if you could come over for a holiday. I could meet you at Edmonton airport and, after a night in a motel, drive you to McBride.'

Just like Jeanna, all details carefully planned. I had no idea that this plan involved her in a round trip of over six hundred miles. We accepted her invitation with great excitement, happy to renew fellowship with this couple whose friendship we had cherished.

McBride is in the heart of the Rockies logging country and at that time had three sawmills working. On our way from Edmonton we saw many huge trucks laden with massive tree trunks but encountered little other traffic on that long, straight highway. Jeanna just drove on and on, keeping up a flow of lively, newsy chatter.

The trees on the mountainsides as we neared McBride defied description - a blaze of yellow and gold in the September sunshine rising almost to the mountain peaks. Our eyes feasted on this beauty just in time. A few days later a sharp frost brought all the leaves down and we would have missed a sight still glorious in my memory.

Most of the McBride houses were made of wood but the bank's house boasted some brickwork and we enjoyed its snug warmth even when frost lay heavy outside.

Jeanna, always busy, left us to amuse ourselves for much of the time and we enjoyed exploring. A massive tree trunk beside a nearby lake became our favourite parking place. The air soon warmed once the sun rose above the mountain peaks and we spent whole mornings looking at the tranquil water and admiring the mountain slopes beyond. I have seldom felt such deep peace and relaxation as I enjoyed seated on that trunk. Large butterflies flitted around us, some a rich velvety brown and orange and others striped in yellow and black.

One day we noticed large bear footprints in the soft ground at the water's edge. After that we found it harder to relax but kept a wary eye open by continually looking over our shoulders. I thought I saw a bear emerging from the bushes a few yards away but it proved to be a black calf coming for a drink.

After those restful days in McBride, Jeanna drove us over five hundred miles to Vancouver to spend five days with Margaret, another mutual friend who had emigrated some years previously. We started that fantastic journey through the Rockies about eight in the morning and arrived after nine the same evening. By then I could not take in one more lovely sight.

While with Margaret we crossed the border into the States for lunch and spent several sunny hours enjoying views of the Pacific coastline. It amused me afterwards to tell friends that I had been to America for the afternoon.

Nearly two years later Douglas and I returned to Vancouver for a coach tour of the Rockies, eager to be charmed once again. I remembered Lake Louise as a sparkling stretch of water, nestling like some huge blue jewel at the foot of surrounding mountains. I longed to savour its beauty again but nature defeated me. I found it covered in ice and surrounded by deep snow. In June! My one disappointment on a fantastic tour.

'Right, we're off to Prince George today,' Robin, our tour leader, told us as we left Jasper.

'Will we be on the highway that passes McBride?' I asked.

'Yes, we stop there for lunch,' she said.

I hastily phoned Jeanna and when we arrived she waved a welcome from the one and only roadside inn. Norrie also joined us for a meal and we valued that special hour with them.

We had booked for that June tour the previous December, when we had no idea we would be flying across the Atlantic again in August. By then Dr. Wirt had retired from editorship of *Decision* but his successor, Roger Palms, invited me to teach at the School of Christian

Writing being held on a university campus in Minneapolis. The invitation both thrilled and challenged me and I accepted eagerly. Typical of their generosity, the Billy Graham Organization also allowed Douglas to accompany me.

When I agreed to become British editorial associate of *Decision* nine years before, nothing could have been further from my mind than an invitation like this. How right my friend June is! Every small thing is part of something bigger.

I worked hard that winter preparing my lessons. I also suffered from a small 'gumboil' which erupted every few days.

'Could it be an abscess?' I asked on my third visit to the dentist.

'With no pain or swelling? No, it's merely a slight infection that will come and go,' he said.

I detected a note of impatience in his voice and felt guilty at bothering a busy man with a minor problem.

The 'gumboil' had persisted throughout our Canadian tour and on our return I felt run-down and low-spirited. I did not tell Douglas as he had problems of his own and faced possible redundancy and subsequent unemployment.

By the time Minneapolis loomed large on my horizon, all earlier enthusiasm had evaporated. I felt incapable of teaching and was tempted to cancel the assignment. It would be so much easier to stay at home than to launch out into the distant unknown.

I reached an all-time low a few days before departure.

'Cancellation is no more than a phone call away,' temptation's voice whispered, yet how could I do that at the last moment? I would fail the school organizers and students alike. What should I do?

Douglas chatted happily about flying to Minnesota as he packed his case and my confusion grew at seeing him so full of anticipation over this new venture. I hadn't the heart to tell him how bad I felt on that black, bleak Monday.

If only I could opt out! I stared at the telephone. Why not lift the receiver and make that transatlantic call? The telephone bell shrilled in my ear, making me jump back.

'Is that you Christine? You've been on my heart all day. Have you a burden?' came a familiar Yorkshire voice.

Who but Mrs Walton would phone like that? Plain. Forthright. Straight to the point.

'I'm supposed to be going to Minneapolis, but feel too low and depressed to make it,' I blurted out. 'I can't teach like this.'

'Of course you must go, dear! Now listen, you're depressed because you're looking within,' my wise friend said. 'Look up, and praise God! He wants to give you a garment of praise in place of that spirit of heaviness, but you have to look up and take it from him.'

'Praising God is the last thing I feel like,' I complained.

'Well, praise him anyway,' Mrs Walton urged. 'And what about God's promises? Aren't you claiming those either?'

Her loving rebuke shamed me. Promise claiming was a long neglected area in my Christian life.

'Fulfil the condition, and here's a promise for you to claim right away,' Mrs Walton continued. '"They that wait upon the Lord shall renew their strength: they shall mount up with wings as eagles; they shall run and not be weary; they shall walk and not faint".'

'The condition sounds like "wait",' I hedged, 'but I can't wait for long because I'm supposed to be going on Thursday, remember.'

'You can begin right now! Let's pray together.'

And pray Mrs Walton did. I listened over the telephone as that prayer winged heavenwards, and words cannot describe how greatly her encouragement lifted my spirits. After that phone call I began looking up instead of wallowing in the mire of despondency into which I had sunk. As I praised God and entrusted myself to his keeping, fears and doubts receded and my faith became wonderfully renewed and strengthened.

Praise still welled up within my heart as Douglas and I settled back in our plane seats a few days later. 'They that wait upon the Lord ... shall mount up with wings as eagles,' Mrs Walton had quoted and my airborne experience reminded me of it, even though the wings bearing me over the Atlantic were those of a Northwest Orient jet, and not of a bird. Spiritually I also soared, sensing that a wealth of new experience awaited me.

I praised God again as the jet touched down in Minneapolis St Paul airport, and thanked him for lifting that 'spirit of heaviness' during the three days that I had waited upon him. Sunshine flooded through the opened plane door and joy flooded my heart at the prospect of all that awaited me out there in the Minneapolis sunshine.

'Hi, there!' an American accent greeted us, and Viola Blake, *Decision's* manuscript co-ordinator, gave us a welcoming hug.

She had driven to the airport to meet us as we were unknown (except through correspondence) to Charette Barta Kvernstoen, organizer of the Writing School, with whom we would be staying for a few days before the school began.

Viola had been our guest on two visits to England and it was good to see her again. Later we enjoyed more of her company as she took us sightseeing round Minneapolis.

Charette's warm welcome also made us feel at home. We felt honoured when she later prepared us a special barbecue meal in her garden. In the daytime we saw little of her since she had all the Writing School arrangements to finalize, but we enjoyed being left to our own devices as we recovered from jet lag and adjusted to the heat.

On my first morning at Northwestern College Campus I rose early to further wait upon the Lord beside beautiful Lake Johanna. Scarcely had I begun to read my Bible when these words in John's first letter arrested my attention: 'If we confess our sins, he (God) is faithful and just to forgive us our sins, and to cleanse us from all unrighteousness.'

It is hard to share deep spiritual experiences, but another promise faced me, with another condition to fulfil prior to claiming it. How that condition convicted me! True, I had begun to wait upon the Lord after Mrs Walton's phone call, but what about the failure of past months? The anxiety and tension, not to mention stupidity at not consulting another dentist about my mouth problem. And what about all the doubts and lack of trust over my husband's threatened redundancy, wondering how we would cope?

All these failings had dishonoured the Lord, yet they remained unconfessed.

'Lord, I'm truly sorry, forgive me. Please cleanse and renew me. Do a new thing in my life,' I pleaded, and God heard my heart cries.

A wonderful sense of Christ's presence and forgiveness engulfed me. The calm waters of Lake Johanna reflected the peace that filled my heart as I returned to the campus buildings, strengthened and enthusiastic to begin my teaching assignment.

Twenty-six warm-hearted, receptive students greeted me. As I looked into their eager, expectant faces I felt greatly concerned not to fail them, and God honoured that unspoken desire. The last traces of fatigue vanished as Christ's power replaced my physical weakness. Like the apostle Paul long ago, I proved that his grace and enabling were indeed sufficient for my need.

Douglas gave me invaluable help and relieved me of extra strain by seeing some of the students who wanted private advice. He dealt with the ones with biographical writing problems, a field of writing outside my experience, but familiar to him.

Inner joy mounted to a climax after the last class, when the students clustered round to hug me.

'We love you for coming so far to teach us,' they said, which so moved me that I had a hard time keeping tears from brimming over.

'You've inspired me to a deeper commitment in my writing,' one girl said.

'Do you know your face glowed while you instructed us?' another asked.

Her question amazed and humbled me. I had gone to Minnesota all too conscious of physical limitations, but those students had seen only Christ's strength, and the outworking of his Spirit. 'God seems to be at his best when his people are at their worst,' C H Spurgeon once said, and I reckoned he must be right.

We flew home on a half-empty plane so I stretched out on the middle seats.

'I'm going to sleep and I don't want to be woken for anything, not anything,' I stressed to Douglas.

And sleep I did, through a violent thunderstorm, loss of plane height, falling chinaware and alarming 'bumps'. Douglas shook me gently when the storm had passed and I opened a sleepy eye.

'I told you I didn't want to be woken,' I grumbled.

'No, but we've just flown over the Isle of Man. We'll be landing in a few minutes.'

I had slept for nine hours, blissfully unaware of the fury of the thunderstorm.

Once home, I paid an emergency visit to another

dentist who X-rayed my mouth. This revealed a long-standing abscess that had spread almost to the sinus area. The dentist extracted a tooth and prescribed penicillin. With that problem at last solved, I soon felt fit and well again.

I could not wait to see Mrs Walton, eager to tell her about my 'Minneapolis assignment'. But on the way to her home God halted me in my tracks. I stood transfixed in the street, astounded at his amazing timing.

An insurance agency had placed an Eagle Star Insurance Company poster outside their premises. It depicted a cloudless blue sky with—what? A majestic eagle aloft on outstretched wings. I wiped away tears of joy and read the caption. Just two words: *Soaring Performance*.

'Oh Lord, how affirming you are!' I choked. 'And yet Minneapolis was all your enabling. Outstretched wings of prayer and praise bore me aloft, but your power provided the thermal currents.'

I hurried on to Mrs Walton's and thanked her for her prayers while I was away.

'Don't expect to always soar in the same way, dear,' she said in her down-to-earth way. 'Sometimes you'll run in your eagerness to serve God in new ways, and when you aren't running you'll be doing your household tasks without fainting.'

Her words did not deflate me. She had not meant them to. Instead I accepted her reminder that sometimes God would just expect me to keep my feet firmly on the ground, in the humdrum of everyday life.

Chapter Fourteen

I am glad I taught at that Writing School because the Billy Graham Organization stopped holding these schools on Northwestern College Campus shortly afterwards. Sadly, I taught at only one more in this country because they too ceased with the discontinuance of the British edition of *Decision*. My editorial work also ended after fourteen rewarding and fulfilling years.

Editors change. Magazines change. Policies change, and my writing life changed again as many of the American magazines for which I had written for so long became closed doors. What should I do next?

God's timing is always perfect and my publishers once again wanted children's books. Readjustment of my writing style took some practice but it felt good to be back with my 'first love'.

Douglas accepted early retirement in the November after we went to Minneapolis. He hung up his suit, changed into jeans and began writing another historical biography. He became so absorbed that he had no time for depression or the other traumas that sometimes beset newly retired people.

Four busy years passed before we again flew across the Atlantic. Back in Vancouver from the Rockies, Norrie and Jeanna invited us to their lovely home. Vancouver hosted the World Exposition that year, with Transport for its theme, and Norrie obtained three-day passes from the bank for Douglas and me.

Exhibitors from the world over presented magnificent displays in huge pavilions but we realised we couldn't see everything so we bought a programme and became selective. We visited the Burmese, Thai, Chinese and Japanese pavilions, as well as the Egyptian, Swiss and many others. Some kept to the transport theme but others gave only a token nod to it, preferring to display their country's carpets and other skilled crafts.

On our third visit we travelled to the far end of the Expo site on a refurbished Mississippi showboat. I noticed a pavilion with an enormous Union Jack painted on its side.

'Patriotism compels me to get off at the next stop and visit the British pavilion,' I said, and Douglas agreed.

That pavilion did full justice to the theme and I felt proud to be British. We looked at an excellent display of transport through the years, from Victorian carriages to fire engines in the thirties and on to the latest in Rolls Royce cars and Underground trains.

'Gee, what a neat "Toob" guide. You couldn't get lost with that,' a woman's nasal tones spoke up over my shoulder, as the speaker gazed at a huge underground map.

'It's a happy thought but unfortunately it's all too easy to go astray,' I told her. 'Even if you've got your colour coding right, you can still travel in the wrong direction.'

'I'd sure like to own a Rolls Royce,' the same friendly lady said later.

'Yes, well they're only owned by the privileged few,' I replied. 'I'd settle for a Mini.'

That evening Jeanna drove us back to the Expo site for a spectacular firework display. Douglas behaved like an excited schoolboy as he watched wide-eyed while one colourful wonder after another either zipped across the water or seemed to erupt like a shower of stars from the river itself.

Near the end of our holiday the pastor of Rose of Sharon Baptist Church, where we had worshipped, called to ask how we had enjoyed our vacation.

'It's been great,' we told him, 'but there's still so much that we haven't seen or done.'

'You'll have to come back,' he chuckled. 'I'll be moving on in a minute, folks. I just stopped by to see you before you leave us.'

I don't know where else Pastor Strauss intended to go that evening but three hours later found him still talking with us. *The Evangelical Doctor*, the biography that Douglas had written on John Wycliffe, had recently been published and the pastor plied him with questions, both about Wycliffe and my husband's writing life.

'And what's your speciality?' he asked, turning to me.

'Children's books, but I'm also interested in writing inspirational and devotional articles. You see, there are so many hurting people around who need uplift and encouragement.'

'I'm glad you care about that,' Pastor Strauss said, 'but don't aim only for the masses. Never forget the ones, Christine. God won't use you in a larger sphere if you forget the ones.'

'Why do you say that?' I asked.

'Because it's something I had to learn early on in my ministry,' Pastor Strauss replied, and I appreciated his frankness. 'I used to dream of preaching to large congregations that would hang onto my every word. I strove to perfect my style to this end, but the Lord halted me in my tracks until I listened to his still, small voice. And that's what he said: "Don't forget the ones in your plans for a world-wide ministry. Don't forget the ones!" '

'I'll remember that. Thanks for sharing it,' I promised.

'If you forget, the good Lord will remind you. He still reminds me that I have a ministry to the ones.'

Pastor Strauss stressed the point so strongly that I knew God meant me to take it in. And he has not let me forget it either. Whenever I have been 'too busy' to send a Get Well card, visit a sick friend, or write to the lonely shut-ins I know, I hear the pastor's German accent: 'Don't forget ze ones, Christine', and it helps me to get my priorities right.

And it is not only the sick or elderly that make up those 'ones'. I have to care about shop assistants too.

After the Canadian visit, friends invited Douglas and me to their wedding anniversary party.

'I'll have to buy some blue shoes to go with my new two-piece,' I told Douglas.

'Okay, you do that while I go to the Post Office,' he replied. 'I'll wait for you outside the shop.'

What a hassle buying one pair of shoes!

'With such incompetent shop assistants, it's a wonder this shop isn't bankrupt,' I snapped, forgetting all I'd ever learned about patience.

The flush on the girl's face deepened as I handed back the excess change she had given me. Then I grabbed my parcel and swung away.

'Why does half the world have to buy shoes on a Saturday?' I muttered, as I fought my way out of the crowded shop.

My husband awaited me outside and I expected a rebuke for taking so long. Instead he asked: 'What's wrong? You look all frayed at the edges.'

So I told him about the irritating salesgirl.

'First, she brought me the wrong shoes, although I had clearly indicated which style I wanted. When she got the style right, she brought me black shoes instead of blue. In the end she produced the right style and colour, but they were the wrong size,' I complained.

Douglas laughed, but I felt too harassed to see the humour.

'That's what comes of leaving things to the last minute,' he commented.

'Right,' I agreed, but inwardly I still heaped blame on that salesgirl.

Home at last, I took my new co-ordinates from the wardrobe and dressed for the party.

The new shoes looked exactly right, yet I felt oddly deflated as I looked at my reflection in the bedroom mirror.

All the evening those shoes mocked me, making it hard to join in the festivities. Each time I looked at them they confronted me with my shortcomings: you were rude to that shop assistant. You could see how anxious she was to rectify her mistakes. You could have been more patient.

I made polite conversation and smiled at the right moments, but inwardly excuses mounted about it being 'one of those days'.

With relief I at last said good night to our hostess. My feet ached, and I could not get the new shoes off fast enough. As I pushed them into a cupboard, I also shut the salesgirl out of my mind and went to bed. But it proved a restless night with only fitful sleep.

Sunday morning our minister was away at a youth camp and we had a visiting preacher. He announced his text from Acts 4: 36: 'Joseph, a Levite of Cyprian birth, who was also called Barnabas by the apostles (which translated means, Son of Encouragement)'.

'The Bible tells us that Barnabas "was a good man, and full of the Holy Spirit and of faith",' the preacher began, 'and I want us to notice how that goodness and faith worked out in his life.'

He explained that Barnabas was generous, courageous, humble and painstaking, yet his greatest gift was encouragement. He had a kind word for all, especially to the slow, the disillusioned, the downhearted, and the failures.

The preacher's words began to flow over my head. Instead of his face, I saw the face of yesterday's flustered shop assistant. Who was I to call her incompetent? How dared I judge her harshly and speak in that impatient, irritable way? Had I forgotten that I was once slow and awkward and considered the dullest pupil in the class?

At ten years of age laziness and lack of attention often got me into trouble. Lessons bored me–until the day that Sister Monique came to the convent school. This young French nun knew little English but she taught us to sew by sitting beside us and demonstrating the stitches. Maybe she sensed my feeling of awkwardness and rejection; she often devoted extra time to teaching me new embroidery stitches.

One day Sister Monique smiled at my handiwork and said: 'It is well, Christine, it is very well.' Those few words in broken English lifted my spirits sky high.

Because Sister Monique encouraged me instead of belittling my grubby, clumsy needlework, I began to work harder in her class and in others. And my school report reflected this improvement.

'Yes, Mark failed miserably, and let Barnabas and Paul down, but Barnabas encouraged him and gave him a second chance,' the preacher raised his voice and jolted me back to the present. 'Had it not been for that Son of Encouragement, Paul could never have later written: *Mark is useful to me in my missionary work.* And who knows, but for the encouragement that Barnabas gave him, Mark may never have written the Gospel that bears his name.'

'Barnabas, obviously a man who cared about the ones as well as preaching to crowds,' I thought.

'You're very quiet,' Douglas said, when we emerged into the sunshine.

'I'm thinking,' I replied. 'I'd never realised that encouragement is one of God's gifts. It costs so little yet it can lift someone from the depths of despair and defeat and give him the courage to press on and try again.'

'Yes, Barnabas did a lot for Mark, didn't he?' Douglas replied, but I was not thinking about Mark.

I was remembering Sister Monique and how my talents had blossomed in the warm climate of her encouragement. I also struggled with straightening out my own attitudes. I knew I owed that shop assistant an apology.

'Encouragement costs so little,' I had said, but in practice that did not prove altogether true. It had cost Barnabas a dissension with Paul, his close friend and co-worker. I, too, needed to heal a breach and apologise before I could offer encouragement to the girl on my heart and conscience.

The next morning pride got in the way, plus a string of excuses why I could not return to the shoe shop. I did the washing on Monday, didn't I? The kitchen floor needed cleaning and the refrigerator awaited defrosting.

These excuses added up to one thing, my reluctance to face that salesgirl. The inner tussle continued and finally drove me to my knees in prayer, a prayer that God answered by giving me the strength of purpose I lacked.

In all the hassle of buying the shoes, I had forgotten to ask for blue shoe cream. My forgetfulness proved a blessing in disguise, for when I returned to the shop, the same girl stepped forward.

'Can I help you, madam?' she asked.

'Yes, but first I want to apologise for being irritable and impatient with you last Saturday,' I replied.

The girl looked puzzled until recollection dawned.

'You ... you don't have to apologise, ma'am,' she said in surprise. 'Why should you when I got everything wrong?'

'It wasn't deliberate. You served me willingly and I know you wanted to please,' I explained. 'Press on, and you'll become an excellent salesgirl. We all learn by experience.'

Stars seemed to shine in that girl's eyes, and her smile set my heart aglow. Did those few words of encouragement, sincerely spoken, make her day? I like to think so. It certainly made mine to pass on encouragement such as I had once received as an awkward school girl.

Dear Pastor Strauss! Sometimes I find it hard to 'remember the ones' with kindness, but I am still working at it.

Chapter Fifteen

Adverse events have sometimes come about so casually that they have taken me by surprise, especially as they have given no initial hint of the trouble that lies ahead. It was like that when I injured my knee while polishing furniture.

The knee complained at the continual getting up and down as I crawled round table and chair legs, but I ignored the pain. It did not occur to me that I had done something serious which would take a full two years to heal.

Usually I enjoyed walking the mile or more to Mrs Walton's home for our Thursday Bible studies, and resented having to ask Joan, one of the group, for a lift. What a blow to my independence! Yet I am glad my swollen knee forced me to do so because I got to know Joan better during those car rides and formed a valued friendship. I came to admire Joan's strong personality and the sincerity that shone from her blue eyes. Although retired, Joan is every inch a nurse still, a caring person who has been of great encouragement to me.

If Joan could not come to a study, then Morwen, another of the group, called for me instead. Small and neat, I have also found a bright and cheerful friend in Morwen. Even when serious illness overtook a member of her family, she still bubbled over with humour and good sense and I appreciate knowing her.

Although so painful and frustrating, a lot of good came out of that knee injury. Perhaps it was an example of the 'all things work together for the good of those that love God' that Paul wrote about.

Apart from deepened friendships, the injury forced me to put the brakes on when I longed to tramp across Epsom Downs or to climb Boxhill. I resented these restrictions but the self-control and discipline that pain enforced served as a useful training ground for further trials beyond the horizon.

When I first attended the Bible studies I left immediately they finished to hurry home and get Douglas some tea before he set off for night work at the international telephone exchange. All that ended when the silicon chip brought about numerous redundancies. After that I could stay for a cup of tea at Mrs Walton's and this sharing time drew me into a close relationship with all the other ladies.

We eight studied and learned a great deal together, with Mrs Walton to guide our thoughts and provide spiritual leadership in the special way that only she could. The more I got to know her, the more I loved and admired her valiant spirit. Despite increasing frailty, she seldom complained and never once cancelled a Bible study, even during a specially difficult time that largely confined her to bed.

Undefeated, Mrs Walton would get up and dress for the Bible study, then rest on top of her bed as we learned together. I doubt if any of us, apart perhaps from Joan, fully appreciated what it cost her in pain, exertion and fatigue, but she certainly won our respect and loyalty. We also absorbed a lot by example as well as from the printed page.

Most of the ladies had cars and one or other of them willingly gave Mrs Walton a lift to the shops, doctor, hospital or chiropodist whenever she needed such transport.

'I wish I could help by taking you about,' I told Mrs Walton, and meant it.

'You visit me instead, dear,' she smiled.

Yet I always felt I gained most from those visits. I often went feeling off colour when colitis flared up, but invariably came away uplifted in body, soul and spirit.

The more time I spent with Mrs Walton, the more she reminded me of Mrs Green, steadfast in spirit, unwavering in faith, and a gifted teacher of the Bible she treasured.

'This is the worst attack of sciatica I've had for a long time,' Mrs Walton told me on one visit.

She did not complain, just stated a fact.

'It must have lasted six weeks,' I sympathised.

'I've prayed often for healing, but God is either saying No or Wait. Meanwhile I'm learning to go through the pain with him,' Mrs Walton said, a smile brightening her pain-drawn face.

'Suffering's a mystery but there must be a purpose in it,' I replied.

It sounded a hollow platitude and I longed to say something of real comfort, but found it hard since her suffering went beyond my experience of pain.

'Yes, suffering is a mystery and we have to leave it with God and, as I said, go through it with him. Deuteronomy 29, verse 29, that's what I repeat to myself,' Mrs Walton said.

Not understanding, I frowned as she reached for her falling-apart Bible.

'"The secret things belong to the LORD our God, but the things revealed belong to us ... that we may follow all the words of this law",' she read. 'You have a questioning mind, Christine, but if you remember this verse it will silence many of those questions and faith will replace them.'

Her eyes twinkled as I inwardly repeated 'Deuteronomy 29: verse 29' to myself. It is a verse I have repeated many times since, when theological Whys have defied answers, or my problems have seemingly had no solution.

Shortly after that visit Mrs Walton gave up leadership of the Women's Meeting at our church. She had a deep love and concern for the many women who attended and it cost her much heartache to relinquish her position because of failing health. She could not attend church on Sundays either since it was too painful for her to sit through a service.

'I long for our Bible studies,' she told me. 'My only real fellowship now is with you ladies.'

A lump rose in my throat when she said that. She gave so much of herself to us and wanted us to mature as Christians and produce spiritual fruit.

****

During the second year after my knee injury the pain

lessened steadily and I looked forward to complete healing. But as my knee improved my general health deteriorated owing to what I assumed to be severe attacks of my 'thorn in the flesh'. Despite these attacks I struggled on with the historical novel I had begun when my knee immobilized me. An American publisher showed an interest in the story, which doubled my enthusiasm. He approved the first three chapters and encouraged me to send the rest of the story as soon as possible.

I worked as hard as my health would permit and posted the finished novel off to America with a sense of triumph and high hopes of publication. Only when I sank back to draw breath did I realise how physically drained I had become.

'This is one of my worst bouts of colitis,' I complained to my husband.

'You've overworked again. I'll get a ball and chain and fasten it to your ankle if you don't ease up,' Douglas threatened.

Visits to the doctor resulted in blood and various other tests which indicated nothing abnormal. I also went to hospital for bowel X-rays.

'Your X-rays reveal a slight diverticular condition,' the doctor told me.

'It sounds awful. What is it?' I asked in bewilderment.

His explanation did not leave me a great deal wiser but I accepted it as the cause of my problems. The months that followed remain a blur of illness, pain and depleted vitality. I did not know it then, but my low condition worried Mrs Walton. She expressed her concern to the Bible study group, all of whom prayed for me regularly.

As more and more activities had to be dropped, I recall being grateful for the discipline of my injured knee. Those restrictions proved good training ground for these new curtailments.

One morning I awoke to the thud of a bulky package on the hall floor. A glance told me that the American publisher had returned my novel. His letter explained that the 'climate' had changed and he no longer required this type of story.

Disappointment. Frustration. Discouragement. These emotions engulfed me as I picked up my scorned manuscript. Not only did I grapple with discouragement but I thought a lot about it.

'Discouragement comes in all shapes and sizes, doesn't it?' Douglas sympathized, and I agreed.

On that bleak Monday morning it came in the shape of a rejected novel, but it comes in other guises and I thought about some of them as I looked out at the wintry scene beyond my bedroom window. I recalled baking a cake that had emerged from the oven more like a soggy pudding.

'I'm hopeless at cooking, what's the use of trying?' the pity-me bird twittered its discouragement.

I washed the front doorstep and within half an hour a van driver, circular distributor and a postman had trampled on it with their muddy shoes. Discouragement made an almost successful take-over bid when the milkman dropped a bottle of milk on the briefly gleaming tiles.

'All that mess when I've just cleaned the doorstep,' I moaned to Douglas.

'It reminds me of an incident in Helen Roseveare's book *Give Me This Mountain*. Do you remember?' he smiled, unruffled.

I nodded, recalling how as a young missionary candidate, Helen's first job in the mission hostel had been to wash the toilet floors. She scrubbed the first toilet but had no sooner begun the second when someone with muddy shoes entered the first. Helen returned to the still-wet floor and washed it again. Meanwhile someone else left footmarks in the second toilet. Helen's superior found her battling with frustration and discouragement.

'For whom are you scrubbing this floor?' she asked.

She helped Helen to see that she was doing it for the Lord.

'And he saw the first time you cleaned the floor. That is tomorrow's dirt,' she said.

Helen records that that piece of quiet, godly wisdom followed her through many years as a missionary.

That same wisdom helped me to get things into proper perspective when my doorstep lost its gleam. Instead of grumbling I did something positive and thanked God that the dropped bottle had not cracked the tiles.

Discouragement is not always that easy to overcome. When my novel thudded onto the floor many questions clamoured for answers. I believed God had called me to be a writer, so why had my novel been rejected, especially when the editor had encouraged me to go ahead with it? Why did I have to be ill when writing it, slowing me down so that I 'missed the boat'?

While searching for answers I came to see that God is far more interested in what I am than in what I do. Patience, so lacking in my make-up, and endurance are qualities that God can produce in me if I will but hand over my disappointments to him. And God did help me to overcome discouragement by widening my horizon to see how, not only Helen Roseveare, but the apostle Paul coped with discouragement and frustration.

At Mrs Walton's Bible studies we noticed how Paul devoted his strength and energy to taking the gospel to Asia Minor, only to find himself cast into Philippian and Roman prisons.

'Do you think he ever asked: "Why, Lord? Why, when there's still so much to do?"' Mrs Walton said, looking at me.

'Well, he must have been fed up. After all he went a long way to take the Good News, so he could be excused for expecting God to keep him out of prison,' I replied.

'Yet look how useful those imprisonments were,' Mrs Walton continued. 'When not sharing the gospel with his guards and with Caesar's household, Paul wrote letters to the Christians in the various cities where he had taught and preached. Those letters form a vital part of the New Testament.'

My spirits lifted as I listened. Paul's letters to the Ephesians, Philippians, Colossians and to Philemon must have instructed, enriched and comforted uncounted believers the world over for nearly two thousand years. But they might never have been written had Paul not been confined in a dungeon. Imprisonment gave him time to pour out his heart to friends in far-away places and we are still benefiting from them!

After that Bible study I felt better equipped to face up to discouragement and disappointment. I also resolved to start writing again. Perhaps one day I would write something that would turn the world upside down!

Chapter Sixteen

At last that difficult year drew to its end and I busied myself with sending off Christmas cards. I popped a note in with the one to my favourite uncle. He had not answered my two previous letters, which made me uneasy.

'Uncle Chris must be about ninety,' I said to Douglas, as I sealed the envelope. 'I expect letter writing's a chore for him and that's why he hasn't written.'

'Phone and wish him a happy Christmas,' Douglas suggested.

I made the long distance call but received only the number unobtainable tone. My uneasiness changed to concern when his usual Christmas cheque did not come. The absence of the cheque did not matter, but my uncle's silence did. What had become of him?

I had loved Uncle Chris since my early childhood. My mother, brother and I sometimes visited my grandfather in Cornwall instead of staying at my aunts' hotel in Torquay. Uncle Chris lived near by and his kindly presence added an extra dimension to those Falmouth holidays.

Distance separated us in later years but my uncle kept in touch by letter and never forgot to send me a Christmas gift.

'I'll have to go to Falmouth to find out what's happened to Uncle Chris and Aunt Ethel,' I said to Douglas when the new year dawned.

'Well you can't go now, the weather's too bad for a long journey, you aren't well enough, and we can't afford the fare or hotel accommodation,' Douglas pointed out, bringing me down to earth with a bump.

'Let's save up and go for Easter,' I suggested.

'You'll have to get well first or the journey will be too much for you,' Douglas replied guardedly.

As Easter drew nearer, Falmouth seemed to recede. Another bout of illness had left me debilitated and Douglas insisted that I should not travel so far. We needed a break but settled for a modestly priced Easter house party in the opposite direction.

'Lord, why must I go to Herne Bay when I particularly want to go to Falmouth?' I fumed.

Hardly a prayer this, more a complaint fostered by doubt.

'God must know I'm anxious, so why didn't he arrange things so that I could go to Falmouth?' I inwardly reasoned. 'Doesn't he care?'

Even on the train to Herne Bay I still fretted about my uncle and aunt. As I stared unseeing out of the window, the years slipped away and I relived those happy childhood holidays in Cornwall. Uncle Chris (who had retired early from work on health grounds) had always been there to play with me, take me out and buy the treats that made those holidays special.

'What about a mug of Horlicks?' he once suggested after a blustery walk round the cliffs - a delicious luxury almost unknown to my brother and me.

The train driver braked sharply, jolting me back to the present problem. When could I go to Falmouth to ask neighbours for news of him?

Instead of anticipating the Herne Bay house party with gratitude, my attitude remained resentful. Uncle Chris was the last living relative on my mother's side of the family and I could not accept the way he had faded out of my life. If God cared as much as I did, why did he allow me to travel in the wrong direction?

'I'm really looking forward to this house party,' my husband's words broke in on my thoughts.

Suddenly I felt ashamed. Preoccupation with my own doubts and wants had blinded me to his needs and what mattered to him. I closed my eyes and prayed for God's forgiveness.

'Lord, I believe you both know and care about my concern over Uncle Chris. Please forgive me for the prayers that have been more of a wail, and help me to accept your timing over going to Falmouth,' I asked.

'I'm looking forward to this house party,' Douglas repeated, studying my face.

'Yes, it's great to get away,' I agreed.

On the first evening at Herne Bay Court, a pleasant, rosy-faced lady sat beside me before the fellowship hour began. We smiled at each other and she introduced herself as Mrs Spargo.

'I live in Truro. Do you know that part of Cornwall?' she asked.

'Not Truro itself,' I replied, with a flicker of interest,

'but I know Falmouth well. My mother grew up there and she used to take me to my grandfather's for holidays.'

'We used to live there too,' my companion beamed, and my interest mounted.

I found myself telling her about my uncle and my longing to go to Falmouth to learn of his welfare.

'Where does he live?' Mrs Spargo asked.

'Dracaena Avenue,' I told her.

'That's where we lived!' she exclaimed.

This was exciting. Incredible. What a small world!

'Did you know Mr and Mrs Robinson?' I blurted out.

'Why, yes. They lived opposite. Such a dear old couple. But then, Mr Robinson died last year aged ninety-one,' Mrs Spargo replied, and for a moment I could only stare at her.

'Since ... since you now live in Truro, how do you know about my uncle in Falmouth?' I stammered, astonished.

'Well, my dear, your aunt Ethel shares a room with my aunt in a Truro nursing home,' Mrs Spargo told me.

My heart sang with relief and joy as she gave me the nursing home address. Who but God, in his wondrous grace, could have arranged our meeting like that? While I worried and fretted, he planned everything to set my mind at rest and to save me the long, expensive journey to Cornwall!

This friendly lady, Mrs Spargo, then told me that she could not stay for the Easter weekend. 'I came to Kent to visit a terminally ill relative in Canterbury Hospital and will be driving home early tomorrow,' she explained.

Praise welled up within me for God's perfect timing. How could I have doubted his care?

'If you only trusted him when you can't see the way ahead you'd save yourself a lot of hassle,' I chided myself.

After meeting Mrs Spargo I wrote to Aunt Ethel regularly. She could not reply since her deformed, arthritic hands prevented letter writing, but when she died, on Maundy Thursday two years later, she left me the brilliant sapphire and diamond engagement ring that Uncle Chris had given to her some seventy years previously.

Much as I value that ring, I treasure even more the evidence of God's loving care.

****

That May the internal problem that had nagged for so long seemed to settle down and Douglas and I went to Christchurch for another short break and change of scenery. The fresh sea breezes, dancing daffodils and burgeoning trees all acted as a tonic. I returned from those few days with more vitality than I had enjoyed for months, not knowing it was but a welcome respite from the undertow of indifferent health.

The following Wednesday I kept wishing I had not eaten a jacket potato for lunch. It had given me violent indigestion pains. The pains increased and I began to vomit. By late evening I groaned in agony and Douglas tried repeatedly to contact our doctor. At long last one of his partners came to examine me. He gave me a morphine injection to ease the pain and looked serious.

'I'm afraid this means immediate hospitalization,' he said.

Just when the going looked good, a painful emergency dominated my horizon.

The doctor arranged emergency admittance to the hospital while Douglas bundled soap, flannel, comb, hankies and a clean nightie into a shopping bag. Since Geoffrey's untimely death hospitals filled me with a morbid dread. Even visiting sick friends sent cold creeps up the backs of my legs. Yet that night I felt quite calm, almost past caring. Anywhere suited me as long as I could be freed from the searing pain.

An ambulance soon came and two strong, kindly men helped me down the maisonette stairs. Where had my strength gone in such a short time?

Douglas came with me in the ambulance and helped with form-filling formalities at the hospital. Morphia had reduced the pain to a dull, aching haze and I felt desperately tired as nurses and house doctors bustled around.

'Right, I'll take you up to the ward now,' one of the nurses told me, after what seemed an interminable wait.

Douglas followed as she wheeled me away.

'There's no point in you coming,' she told him and my heart went out to him standing in that corridor in the middle of the night.

'I suppose I'll have to walk home,' he said to another nurse and I suddenly felt guilty over the trouble I was causing.

'You can ring for a mini cab. I'll get you the number.'

The voice faded beyond earshot but it relieved me to know that Douglas would not have to walk the four miles home at two o'clock in the morning.

The nurse took me up to a private room beside the surgery ward. I was fortunate to be admitted that night, that being the only vacant bed.

Another doctor questioned me, more nurses glided silently in and out bringing, among other things, a stand, saline drip bag, and plastic tubing. One nurse pushed a small plastic tube up my nose. It jammed in the nostril and I cried with the pain. She tried the other nostril and the tube went on down my throat to my stomach. The nurse also inserted a second tube into a vein on the back of my left hand, and hung a notice over the bed which said: Nothing by mouth.

'Don't lift your arm up, or the drip won't flow,' she said, her dark skin accentuating the whiteness of her teeth when she smiled.

With that friendly warning she departed, leaving me too exhausted to reflect on the suddenness of my arrival or to wonder what would happen next.

During the next four days I performed acrobatic feats getting out of bed and going the short distance to the toilet. With my left hand I guided the wheeled stand attached to me by the drip tube. In my right hand I held the bag attached to the tube up my nose.

Washing presented problems and required careful planning as I feared dislodging a tube. After two days I became more venturesome and tried to change my night-dress and put on the bedjacket that Douglas had brought me. This required even more careful manoeuvring but my brain became too fuddled to cope. Should I unhook the drip bag and push it through the nightdress sleeve? And what about pushing it through the bedjacket sleeve before pulling the nightie over my head?

The plastic drip bag looked dangerously fat for this operation. Rather than burst it, perhaps it would be better to wait until there were more drips in me and less in the bag. I waited an hour but the bag had not slimmed much, so impatience got the better of me. I pulled my arm out of my nightie sleeve, tried to push the bag after it, then panicked. The tube from the back of my hand began to fill with blood.

'Nurse! Nurse!' I yelled, pressing the emergency button.

A young Irish nurse quickly took in the situation.

'Sure now, what a mess you're in!' she chuckled.

She had caught me half naked, still struggling with my nightie. She deftly freed me from the tangle of tubing that prevented me from getting it off and helped me into the fresh nightie and bedjacket.

'Now we can put the drip bag back on its hook,' she said. 'That way the fluid will flow in the right direction.'

'Bag up, arm down,' I reminded myself sheepishly as I slid back into bed.

****

Douglas came each afternoon and I longed for his visits. He showed no shock at the tubes up my nose and in my hand but later told me that they frightened the wits out of him.

'I can't eat or drink until this nasal tube's removed, but the pain's almost gone, so it's worth it,' I said.

'Do they know what caused the pain?' Douglas asked, his voice anxious.

'If they do, they haven't said yet. People keep coming for blood and other samples, so they're working on it,' I replied.

'You're lucky to have this room to yourself,' Douglas remarked, looking out of the window.

'It's great. I slept most of this morning and a nurse told me she came back three times to get a sample. Nice of her not to wake me up.'

Douglas, always thoughtful, bought me two little books, well-illustrated with not too much text. One was about wild flowers and the other about butterflies, and I loved those books. I also had a Gideon New Testament in my locker and enjoyed reading the Psalms included at the back of it.

****

'Just taking you down to the ultrasonic scanner,' a porter said on my second day, and he transferred me from the bed to a long wheeled trolley.

The saline drip stand and bile gauge bag had to come too. How I hated the tubing and longed for its removal from my nose and hand!

The next day both tubes were taken out and I could

drink freely from the water jug beside my bed. Never had water tasted so good. That afternoon Joan, my Bible study friend, drove Douglas to the hospital, which saved him waiting for two infrequent buses. She also brought good wishes from all the ladies in the group.

'We're praying for you,' she said cheerfully, 'and Mrs Walton especially sends you her love.'

The following morning one of the doctors came to see me and I looked at him expectantly. Had he come with the test results?

'As I suspected, you have an infected gall bladder,' he told me, calm and straight to the point. 'I advise its removal otherwise it could give you a lot of trouble later on.'

Infected gall bladder! An operation! My mind reeled.

'There ... there's nothing wrong with my bowels, then?' I asked. 'No cancer or anything?'

'Definitely not, but you'll be better off without your gall bladder,' he repeated. 'We can't operate now, but I suggest you rest up at home and we'll send for you when we have a bed available.'

The chance to go home delighted me, but the implications of a major operation took longer to sink in. My appendix had been removed in this hospital when I was eighteen and my memories of that operation hardly filled me with enthusiasm for another, more serious one.

The Irish nurse brought me bread and butter for tea that day and it tasted like a banquet. The pain returned slightly after eating it but I said nothing in case the pain prevented me from going home.

The ward sister, warm-hearted and kind, gave me a diet to keep to and I scanned it ruefully. Since childhood I had drunk a daily pint of full cream milk but the diet allowed only fat-free skimmed milk. I had also eaten a dozen eggs a week, but the quota dropped to three. I loved Canadian cheddar cheese but had to settle for fat reduced cheese which seemed tasteless by comparison.

Morwen, bright and cheerful as usual, drove Douglas to the hospital with my clothes and kindly took us home. Only when I walked to the hospital lift did I realise how weak I had become. But weakness did not prevent me from thanking God for the friends who rallied round to help, or to encourage with letters, cards and flowers.

It felt good to be in my own bed again, yet that night I could not sleep. So much had happened so quickly, and the operation loomed large and threatening. I also had a pain again after Douglas gave me tomato soup for tea.

'Breakfast in bed for you,' Douglas said the next morning.

He brought me a few grapes and a small helping of porridge topped with skimmed milk. I lay back after that meagre meal and gazed through half-closed lids at the picture of Brixham harbour that hangs on the bedroom wall. My thoughts wandered down memory lane to the day that Douglas bought that picture, the day I nearly did not go to Brixham.

'We don't have to go,' Douglas had said, his voice gentle and understanding.

I had wavered, afraid to spoil our holiday by revisiting

172

the small fishing town where I had once been so happy. Although several years had passed, memories remained sharp and I feared being hurt. I watched some Scandinavian students board the ferry and, on a sudden impulse, followed them. These carefree youngsters sang all the way across the calm, blue waters of Torbay and their clear, harmonious voices helped to relieve the tension building up inside me.

While I watched Torquay fade into the distance some partly remembered words that Paul wrote to the Philippians floated into my mind: 'Forgetting those things which are behind, and reaching forth to those things which are before, I press toward the mark for the prize of the high calling of God in Christ Jesus.'

The challenge of the high calling of God had often thrilled me but that day the first phrase about forgetting confronted me. How could I forget or pretend the painful past was not still bound up in the fabric of my being? Silently I prayed for strength and courage to face the day.

The crossing ended all too soon. Douglas smiled reassuringly as he helped me off the ferry and I tried to hide my cowardice. We walked along the quayside, where I glanced up at the quaint, slate-roofed cottages perched on the hillside. With a pang I recalled the maze of narrow streets, brightly painted doors, and green glass floats hanging in some windows.

The last time I came to Brixham Geoffrey had been with me. We had explored those byways together and felt we were stepping back into the days of smugglers, brandy kegs and laden ponies trotting through the dark. We had been married for seven years and that holiday had been special, like a second honeymoon.

Memories receded as Douglas slipped my hand under his arm. We looked at the fishing boats moored along the quayside and watched seagulls wheeling overheard. Then my gaze went beyond the harbour towards the flats where Geoffrey and I had spent that other holiday and tears pricked behind my eyes.

Some old men, wrinkled and wise in the ways of the sea, sat mending their nets close by, and Douglas paused to watch as they worked with strong, skilful hands.

'Nothing changes here,' I said.

It was true enough. The sights and smells were exactly as I remembered them, only my life had changed. I recalled with a stab of pain the evening when Geoffrey and I had stood on the flat balcony to watch the sea deepen from liquid amber to blood red, and how some inner foreboding had made me shiver as we went indoors. Geoffrey had died a few days later.

'Look both ways!' Douglas jolted me back to the present.

We crossed the road to a small gift shop, and I saw the picture of Brixham harbour in the window. I liked it so much that Douglas suggested buying it. I hesitated. Did I really want that picture to remind me of the bitter-sweet of Brixham? While I stood undecided, Douglas went in and bought it.

'Where shall we go now?' he asked. 'Would you like

to see the holiday flats, or would you rather look at some more shops?'

In a moment of panic I wanted to escape from Brixham altogether, but my husband's kindly support both calmed and encouraged me, and he appeared not to notice the beads of perspiration I could feel on my forehead. I shrank from seeing those flats, so poignant with memories, yet I did not want the fear of inner pain to win the day. The purpose of coming to Brixham had been to overcome fear.

'Yes, let's go to the holiday flats,' I blurted out, before a surge of courage evaporated.

My heart thudded as we skirted the harbour and rounded a bend in the road. Suddenly there they stood, white and sunbathed, just as I remembered them. My eyes went straight to the top balcony where Geoffrey and I had watched the sun go down.

It hurt my eyes to look for long in the strong sunlight, yet I felt no inner pain, only a deep sense of peace. The heartache I dreaded did not come. With awe and relief I found that by facing the ordeal of coming to Brixham I had, unknowingly, also overcome the fear phantom that had suggested the sight of those flats would distress me. Although time had largely healed the wounds of grief, I still needed to face up to this emotional challenge.

In that enlightening moment I understood that God wanted me to live positively and joyfully, unafraid of dark shadows from the past. He also wanted me to do as Paul urged - to reach forward to those things which are before, pressing on in faith and trust in my loving heavenly

Father. I had allowed a lurking fear to overshadow an otherwise bright present and blur my vision of the high calling of God.

Did this new understanding mean that I must completely blot out the 'things that were behind'? No! Precious memories would always be locked in my heart's treasure chest. From time to time I could lift the lid and peep again at past love and happiness, but I should not long to recapture them or be distressed at the impossibility of doing so. Such memories should enrich the present and encourage me to put the most into each fleeting moment. That was the way to live a victorious Christian life and press towards the mark for the prize that Paul wrote about.

My footsteps were light as Douglas and I crossed the road to climb onto the wall that protected the harbour. With a new eagerness I walked towards the lighthouse at the far end.

'Happy now?' Douglas asked.

I smiled, grateful for the sympathetic perception he had shown. He stood by the lighthouse with the picture of Brixham tucked under his arm, and it pleased me that we would be taking it home. If ever I was tempted to do too much 'looking back', that picture would remind me that it is by reaching forward and pressing on that faith and trust are rewarded.

Lying in bed after breakfast that morning, I sighed as I continued to look at the scudding clouds in the picture. My sentiments had been good the day Douglas bought it, but now I did not feel much like reaching forward towards a major operation. Yet somehow that picture strengthened and encouraged and I found myself thinking that maybe God sometimes allows adversity to creep up on us on rubber-soled shoes so that we will cast ourselves more fully upon him.

Even in my weakness, confidence welled up within and I knew that whether the trouble should be physical, spiritual or emotional, God would be sufficient for my need and he would see me through.

Chapter Seventeen

Douglas and I had planned to stay at Netherhall Christian Guest House in Largs that June. We looked forward to our first visit to Scotland, but, of course, we could not go. Every day we waited for the letter that would tell me when I should return to hospital.

Meanwhile I was supposed to rest, but all my old impatience reasserted itself. If I must have this operation, why couldn't I have it quickly and get it over, instead of uncertainty dragging on day after day? As well as fretting, I also hoped and prayed that I would be given the same private room. Selfish of me, perhaps, but I did not relish being close to other patients' moans, groans and snores.

'I'll cope much better on my own,' I told Douglas, and I kept telling God the same thing as well.

After three weeks the longed-for envelope slipped through the letter-box.

'I'm going in on Monday week,' I announced.

Hardly an exciting prospect, but it did end the uncertain waiting.

A few days later Dorothy Wicker, one of our church elders' wives, called to talk and pray with me and I appreciated her visit.

'Are you afraid of death?' she asked in a quiet, matter-of-fact voice.

'No, not at all,' I replied, with an inner assurance that surprised me.

How could I be afraid when my Saviour would welcome me to a far better home? A thrill, almost of exultation, passed through me.

I might not be able to echo fully Paul's words: 'For me to live is Christ,' but I did know, as Paul affirmed, that 'to die is gain'. Gain! I tried to visualize the joy of being in Christ's presence forever, free from pain, weariness and sickness. More important, free to worship God more fully and to praise him as he should be praised.

Of course I valued my life here, even treasured each day as a God-given gift. I would be happy to stay, if possible in better health, yet it reassured and strengthened me to discover that death held no dread. As Geoffrey had done before me, I would simply pass beyond the horizon of human sight.

On the Sunday night, Douglas and I prayed together as we always do at bedtime.

'Father, I commit Christine into your loving hands,' Douglas prayed, 'and ask that you will give skill to the surgeon, doctors and nurses so that this operation will be successful and Christine will come safely home again.'

As Douglas prayed I knew that my greatest regret in passing from this life would be leaving him alone. If that happened, I hoped that God would give him another companion, as he had given Douglas to me after Geoffrey died.

Somehow it seemed unreal going off to hospital. Apart

179

from carrying an already crammed shopping bag to the bus stop, instead of an empty one, I could have been going to the shops. With all the hospital admittance formalities completed, I at last reported to the surgical ward sister.

'Your bed is ready,' she said briskly.

We walked up the corridor towards the private room. No! What had gone wrong? She turned aside into the main ward and my spirits plummeted. She indicated the middle bed of three on the left and suggested that I undress in the washroom.

I dumped the shopping bag onto the bed, whizzed back the zip and pulled out my nightie and dressing-gown. As I did so I felt that God had let me down.

'Hello, are you taking my place?' a cheery voice greeted me in the washroom. 'That bed didn't stay empty for long, then.'

A small, wiry woman in her early sixties grinned at me while pulling on her tights.

'I'd hoped for a private room,' I blurted out.

'You'd be lucky,' she grinned even more widely, revealing several gaps in her teeth. 'What are you in for anyway?'

'Gall bladder removal,' I told her.

'That's what I've had. Want to see my gallstones?'

Before I could reply she showed me a small, transparent container full of jagged, reddish-brown stones. I shuddered at the sight.

'You must have been in pain with those sharp things inside you,' I sympathized.

'Want to see my scar an' all?' this lively little person offered.

She promptly hauled up her vest to reveal a long, ugly scar under her right ribs. Horrified, I shivered with fright.

'So ... so that's what they'll do to me,' I gulped.

'Nothing to it,' my companion grinned. 'In and out of here in nine days, that's what. Good luck, luv. Enjoy your stay!' and off she breezed.

The next morning the lady to my right was removed to the non-surgical ward and later a plump-faced, grey-haired lady took her place.

'I'm Iris,' she said, and we became instant friends.

Did our shared crisis draw us like a magnet? At first I thought so. The memory of the wiry lady's horrible scar still haunted me and it dawned on me that at a time like this I needed the help and reassurance of companionship. I even conceded that God knew what he was doing by putting me with five other women. I endorsed that opinion more fully during the next few days, when I learned a lot more about suffering.

Iris wore a dressing-gown of the same material and almost identical colour to mine. It differed only in style. But I soon discovered that we had something far more important in common. We shared our Christian faith. No wonder we had felt drawn to one another!

'We'll pray for each other every evening, shall we?' Iris suggested, placing her Bible on her bedside locker, and I willingly agreed.

That night a fifteen-year-old girl came to the bed on

my left for emergency appendix surgery. After her operation we learned that she was a Roman Catholic, and we included her in our prayers. We also prayed for the three ladies on the other side of the ward, two of whom I privately nicknamed The Gripers because they constantly complained.

'I'm having my gall bladder out tomorrow,' I told Iris. 'The surgeon's coming to see me this morning. I'll be glad to get it over.'

'I've got cancer and am having my breast off, probably on Friday,' Iris replied.

'Cancer! You sound wonderfully calm about it,' I said.

'It's my faith, dear. I don't collapse in a heap when trouble comes. My times are in God's hands, you see,' Iris replied.

'You've got the same trust and confidence that David had when he wrote his psalm,' I said, taking the Gideon New Testament from my locker.

I turned to the back of it and found Psalm 31.

'Let your face shine on your servant,' I read. 'But do you know something? When you quoted the fifteenth verse just now your face glowed. It's great to see your faith in action. I'm also glad that God didn't let me have the private room I wanted. I'm strengthened by having you beside me.'

'Mutual encouragement, that's what we're giving,' Iris smiled.

The surgeon came and questioned me. He also read the

medical record hanging at the foot of my bed, and stroked his chin thoughtfully.

'We'll operate on Friday,' he said, and my heart sank.

Mentally and emotionally I had schooled myself for that operation the next day but now had to keep myself boosted up for another three days.

'Patience, dear. Patience!' Iris said, when she saw my frustration. 'Your times are in God's hands too, aren't they now?'

I deserved that gentle admonition and admired Iris for being frank with me. But two days later I could not help envying her when a hospital porter wheeled her away for her surgery a day early. Why couldn't it have been me? At least I had the grace to pray for her and watched with relief when she was later returned to her bed, serene in her unconsciousness.

Visiting time ended at five o'clock and, after Douglas had gone, Thursday evening and the long night hours stretched before me. I slept only fitfully because the patient in the window corner kept rattling the rail fastened to her bed, waking the rest of us up. She did this whenever she wanted attention, even if it was only that her tissue box had fallen to the floor.

As I lay awake in the small hours, God spoke to me in the semi-darkness: 'Be strong and very courageous ... be not afraid, neither be thou dismayed: for the LORD thy God is with thee whithersoever thou goest.'

In his wisdom and tender love he brought to my mind the very words that had both comforted and strengthened me when Geoffrey died. Now they reassured me that 'whithersoever' included the operating theatre.

My last prayer before surgery was: 'Thank you, Lord, that my times are in your hands.' With my heart resting on that pillow of peace, I drifted off into unconsciousness.

Morphine injections relieved the blur of pain and discomfort during the next three days. Douglas came each afternoon although talking tired me. We simply sat in companionable silence.

'Is my wife all right?' he later told me he had asked the staff nurse, 'only her voice seems very weak.'

'Well, she has had a major op, but she'll soon be okay,' the nurse reassured him.

But it did dismay me to discover just how weak I had become. The recurrent illness of the previous two years had undermined my stamina so that the operation took more of a toll than it should have done.

Added to the drip tube in my hand, I now had a bigger one draining from my stomach into a bag hung beside the bed. Weakness did not deter me from being mobile and experience gained during my previous hospital stay helped when it came to negotiating the wheeled stand and tubes. Sometimes I unhooked the drip bag from the stand and carried it muttering: 'Bag up, arm down' as I went, but this proved difficult when washing or performing natural functions.

On the third morning after surgery I ventured down to the far end of a long corridor. It seemed like a ten-mile walk in the effort it required. A picture faced me at the end of the corridor, a delightful autumn scene with sunlight shafting through golden-leafed trees. Physically and mentally I felt at complete ebb tide. With nothing specific to cry about, I sobbed as I tried to look at that colourful painting. Weakness almost defeated me as I held the corridor rail for support.

'You'll never be strong enough to walk in woodland again,' the pity-me bird twittered and tears flowed in a renewed flood.

I thought of the cross-country walks that Douglas and I had begun to enjoy again, day outings to Brighton or Portsmouth, and the keep-fit class I had cautiously rejoined. Now they would all have to go.

'You've got to *be* fit to keep fit,' the pity-me bird mocked.

I turned slowly from the painting with its shafting sunbeams and golden hues. That sunlight, too, seemed a hollow mockery now that a grey blanket of depression hung heavily upon me.

It's amazing how sentences from the past can slide from one's memory bank at times like that. I suddenly recalled a friend of my Exclusive Brethren days whose husband, barely thirty, fell seriously ill with double pneumonia.

'I believe the Lord will take him home,' Eloise told me, her grey eyes solemn.

'How can you say that so calmly?' I asked.

'It's much better if you accept it,' Eloise replied, her voice low, trusting and submissive.

I proved the truth of her words when Geoffrey died some years later, and now they rang in my ears again as I paused to rest half-way up the corridor.

'Lord, I do accept what's happened to me,' I prayed. 'I also accept that I'll never be strong enough to walk in the woods again. All I ask is that I'll be able to run my home and do the shopping.'

That prayer sounds pathetic now, but I meant every word. I truly did accept what I believed to be my lot, and acceptance brought peace.

Back in the ward, one of the patients noticed my red-rimmed eyes.

'You look as if you've got the down-and-out-blues,' she observed, 'but hang on, it will soon pass. It's all the stuff they pump into you. I don't hold with all that dope myself.'

My spirits did perk up within a day or two and when I once again walked up the corridor, I actually smiled at that woodland scene with its tints of copper, yellow and gold. And this time the sunlight dancing on the leafy path became a symbol of hope of brighter days ahead, rather than of despair. The low ebb-tide in my life had turned and started to rise again.

Chapter Eighteen

Iris had her stitches out a few days after my operation, with the promise of going home at the weekend.

'Fortunately we had to remove far less tissue than anticipated, thanks to you noticing the lump early on,' the surgeon told her, and Iris smiled her pleasure that she still had two breasts.

'I'm happy for you, but I'll miss you when you go,' I told her, yet my words hardly conveyed the void I knew I would feel.

I longed for the tubes to be removed from my hand and side and the time came at last. First the nurse took the tube from my hand and wheeled the empty drip bag away. She returned with a small glass.

'Drink just one glassful of water an hour,' she told me.

'What about the tube in my side? Can't that come out too?' I asked.

'Not yet. What a hurry you're in!' the nurse replied in her lilting Irish brogue.

Those tiny glassfuls of water tasted like nectar and I longed for more, but that presented problems. I soon found that I could neither eat nor drink weak tea without being sick. I envied one of the Gripers opposite who reacted to the same surgery in an entirely different way. This patient had one meal a day which lasted all day long.

Her daughter brought her reinforcements to supplement the 'lousy hospital food' in the shape of Swiss rolls, sausage rolls, trifles, chocolate biscuits and other snacks which the Griper stowed away in her locker.

When a nurse wheeled this patient away for a bath (with the aid of a special lift contraption), the Irish nurse took the opportunity to tidy her locker.

'For sure now, what a larder this patient has!' she exclaimed, and her cheeks dimpled into a smile as she tried unsuccessfully to put some other things in the locker.

'She's a proper rubber tum, that's what,' the other Griper told her, and the name stuck.

Upon her return from the bath, the rest of us teased Rubber Tum about her larder.

'Well, I've got to get me strength up, haven't I?' she said, munching a biscuit.

Her new nickname, of which the Irish nurse had jokingly informed her, amused her and she patted her large abdomen without embarrassment as she reached for a jam tart.

Iris should have left the hospital before my sickness problem developed, but her scar turned septic and delayed her.

'What a shame that's happened, but it's great for me to still have you beside me,' I told her.

'If you don't soon stop being sick they'll have to put you back on that drip,' Iris replied.

Whether it was the shock of that threat, or just the

psychological effect of her words, I don't know, but the next slice of bread I ate stayed down, as did some cornflakes the following morning.

The ward sister took my stitches out as she wished to teach a new technique to a trainee nurse. Later another nurse removed the tube from my side. What bliss! I had feared pulling that tube out accidentally, but need not have worried. It proved reluctant to leave me.

'We're making good progress, the vomiting having stopped,' the doctor said on his next round. 'We can now think in terms of going home. How would you feel about Sunday?'

'That's fine. I've a friend who can come for me on a Sunday,' I enthused.

'You'll feel washed out for a couple of weeks so rest and take things quietly,' the ward sister advised.

'Did sister say two weeks? I've heard it takes two years to get over a gall bladder op,' Rubber Tum said later, through a mouthful of Mars bar.

'Two years! Horrors! I hope not,' I exclaimed.

On Sunday I kissed Iris a fond farewell. Morwen, bright and cheerful, brought Douglas to the hospital and drove us both home. Home! Away from the antiseptic atmosphere of that surgical ward.

Becoming mobile and getting my muscles into full working order proved a slow process. I chafed at these limitations but found that times of adjustment can be growing times too.

At first I failed to see the physical restrictions as part

of God's cutting back and pruning, so I felt frustrated when sorting out old receipts and other obsolete papers. I could not tear up paper for long without getting a sharp, cramp-like pain in my right side. Knitting presented problems for the same reason.

Morwen called and found me still resenting my immobility. She listened to my complaints then said: 'Not only must you learn to accept your limitations but to know them, which isn't the same thing, and harder to do.'

I needed to hear her say that, but I also prayed for increased strength. As I prayed I came to see that God does not immediately change disagreeable circumstances just because I am his child. Instead he changes me, if I will let him.

My Bible, lying on the window-sill, invited me to pick it up. I turned the pages at random and found myself reading Ecclesiastes, where one verse came vibrantly alive: 'He (God) has made everything beautiful in its time. He has also set eternity in the hearts of men; yet they cannot fathom what God has done from beginning to end.'

I read and reread those words and they throbbed with ever more vitality and truth. They also breathed comfort into my weary heart.

I might not understand the mystery of God's ways, and I certainly did not understand the mystery of suffering, yet I recognized that all this pain and feebleness need not be pointless. God both could and would make it beautiful in its time. It would bring forth a harvest of fruit, the enduring fruit of his Holy Spirit, transforming my character into greater Christ-likeness.

With a growing sense of awe I asked: more of Christ's love and compassion? More of his patience, endurance and self-control? More kindness and gentleness? The furrowing and ploughing of pain appeared a high price but then, as I also asked myself, has there ever been even a material harvest that is not costly in time, patience and back-breaking effort?

'Lord, I understand. It's the same with spiritual fruit, isn't it?' I whispered. 'And if you'll really make all this beautiful in its time, then it's infinitely worthwhile. I won't ask again that you'll take away the pain and inability, but just that you'll go through it with me.'

And as I prayed I felt the God of all comfort draw very close.

I wish I could say that this was a once and for all victory over my problems and swinging emotions, but life is seldom that easy, nor are battles so quickly won. I made some good discoveries though, not least of which was that God is wonderfully patient and Today is not the limit of his working time.

****

As a child I often paused on the way home from school to stare up at an advertisement high on the side of a building. This hoarding displayed a huge picture of a blue sea capped with white waves. A ruddy-faced man dressed in striped pyjamas sat astride an outsize Bovril jar that tossed in the choppy water. The caption underneath read: 'Bovril prevents that sinking feeling.'

Unfortunately Bovril could not prevent the type of sinking feeling against which I struggled.

'You'll never be any good for anything. You're useless,' I told myself.

While still grappling with my impotence, some words from the fortieth psalm came to my aid, words that I didn't even know I had committed to memory: 'I waited patiently for the LORD; and he inclined unto me, and heard my cry. He brought me up also out of an horrible pit, out of the miry clay, and set my feet upon a rock, and established my goings.'

I could hardly claim a patient wait, yet in his grace the Lord did hear my cries and helped me onto firmer ground where rest and sunshine slowly performed their healing tasks.

While resting I meditated on the different methods God uses to comfort and encourage. Sometimes he draws close himself, while at others he uses friends to either visit, phone or write.

'If you don't take it easy now, you'll suffer for it later on,' Joan, the ex-nurse, warned when she came, which reinforced what Morwen had already told me.

'I hate being so useless,' I complained.

'Well, I'd suggest you set yourself daily targets to aim at, just small, easy tasks at first but enough to give you a sense of achievement,' Joan advised. 'Gradually you'll find you can do more. And be sure to have a daily walk, won't you? Outdoor exercise is a great lifter of drooping spirits.'

I accepted her advice, grateful for such a wise and caring friend.

And I will never forget the day when the telephone shrilled and Douglas called me to come quickly.

'It's an international call ... Canada,' he said, handing me the receiver.

'Is that Christine Wood? ... Hold the line, please. I have a personal call for you,' the Canadian operator said.

Bewildered, I held on. Could it be Jeanna in Vancouver?

'Hello there, Christine. I'm calling from Bowood Gospel Chapel, Calgary and my name's Donna,' a lady said. 'We're shortly holding a ladies' retreat when our subject will be *The Inner Beauty of a Christlike Character*. We'll be considering holiness and right attitudes. That's where you can help us, if you will. Your article *Right Shoes, Wrong Attitude* is just right for in-depth study. Do I have your permission to reprint for all the ladies present?'

With a quick mental flip I recalled the article I had written for *Decision* about that frustrating shopping trip when I wanted a pair of blue shoes.

'Why yes, you're welcome to use my article,' I replied. 'I'm delighted that it will help you.'

Donna thanked me, then said: 'I've never made a transatlantic call before. It feels good to call someone in England. How are you, Christine?'

'Well actually, I'm recovering from a major operation and finding it hard going,' I told her.

'Thank you for sharing that, honey. Not only will we use your article, but we'll include prayer for your well-being on our retreat agenda.'

The psalm that I had vividly recalled continues: 'And he has put a new song in my mouth, even praise unto our God.' How my heart sang as I replaced the receiver! Those ladies, none of whom I'm likely to meet this side of heaven, were nevertheless my spiritual sisters, members of God's family of believers, and they would care enough to pray for me at their retreat.

'Only God could take an incident in a small shoe shop and give it the international value of use at a Canadian retreat,' I said to Douglas.

'And he'll use you and your writing again, you'll see,' he replied.

'Isn't God's timing marvellous? That call came just when I needed a boost,' I said. 'He makes everything beautiful *in its time*. Solomon wrote that, and I'm learning the truth of it.'

Chapter Nineteen

'How about returning to the Bible study?' Joan asked, several weeks later. 'I'll give you a lift if you'd like to try.'

I accepted Joan's offer and Mrs Walton welcomed me back with a loving hug.

'We're studying Paul's letter to the Philippians,' Mrs Walton told me and, as I listened to all that we shared, I felt I could not have returned at a better time.

'We've talked about Paul's imprisonments before. He wrote this letter while in a Roman prison,' Mrs Walton continued. 'In the letter he told the Philippians that he hoped to send Timothy to them that he might come back with first hand news of their spiritual welfare. "For," as Paul wrote, "I have no one else who is like-minded in his genuine care for you ...".'

'Titus also brought Paul news from Corinth. I was thinking about that only recently,' I added.

'Yes, Paul longed for news of the many churches he could no longer visit,' Mrs Walton agreed.

'So much loving and caring on Paul's part, yet what eventually happened? Didn't he later write to Timothy saying: "All in Asia have forsaken me"?' Peggy asked.

This sad reminder led us to think about the seven churches mentioned in the first chapters of Revelation.

'They've all gone, their lampstands removed, as the

apostle John warned,' Peggy continued, 'yet Paul's lifework wasn't wasted, least of all his imprisonments. Perhaps he sometimes felt frustrated and prayed: "Lord, there's a whole world out there to evangelize. You know I want to go to Spain ... but all I can do is write letters."'

'But what letters!' Morwen exclaimed.

'Many of those early church towns no longer exist. They are just historical names, yet we still have Paul's letters,' Mrs Walton smiled. 'When he thought he was doing least, he actually did most in terms of what has lasted. And, you know, that could well be true of us too.'

I drank in every word, feeling they were just for me. In my heart I praised God for the wisdom of his ways, inwardly praying: 'Please, Lord, do with my time as you see best, and give me the grace not to resent my limitations.'

'See how God can use what we call limitations,' Mrs Walton said, just as if she could read my thoughts.

'I'm glad we've talked about this again today. I really needed to hear it,' I replied.

'It's been the Spirit's guidance,' Mrs Walton beamed.

****

For many years I have been an avid reader of *Every Day With Jesus,* the Bible study notes written by Selwyn Hughes. Because of my interest in Selwyn's ministry I became a Prayer Partner shortly after my operation–one of those 'little things' that became part of a bigger thing.

Selwyn had long dreamed of running a Christian

Training Centre specializing in counselling and leadership skills. But where could he find suitable premises? One memorable day Selwyn looked at Waverley Abbey House, near Farnham, which was up for sale. He was convinced that this eighteenth century Georgian house, surrounded by lawns and woodland, exactly met his purposes and his organization, Crusade for World Revival, made an offer.

This offer received priority over more favourable ones and, after payment of the initial deposit, gifts poured in from Christians far and wide to meet the remainder of the cost price. The house required extensive renovation and refurbishment but three years later, in August 1987, the doors opened and the lovely old house lived again - as a Christian Training Centre.

Two years later Douglas and I went to a Partners' Weekend and wandered from one tastefully furnished room to the next, thrilled with God's goodness in providing such a magnificent house for Selwyn's purposes. We caught the vision of all that could be achieved in these delightful surroundings.

The partners present opened their hearts to one another that weekend. We shared our joys and sorrows, hopes, fears and problems in a frank and open way, and I shared my still-present feeling of uselessness.

'I'm supposed to be a writer but creativity has died and I'm battling with physical and mental burnout,' I complained.

On the Sunday morning we shared in a simple Communion service, after which a friendly, blue-eyed man came to sit beside me.

'Your face came vividly before me while I prayed last night,' he said, 'and God has laid it on my heart to tell you that he has a wider sphere of service for you than you've had before. Just be patient and await his timing.'

This man spoke with such loving assurance that I felt too choked to even thank him for speaking to me.

The weekend passed all too quickly and later I asked myself: Could what that man said be true? Is God really going to use me again? If so, when? I'm still so limited.

About a week later an American friend sent me a hardback book of daily meditations by Billy Graham. At first I reacted negatively.

'Now there's a man with impact. He's really achieved something in his life, while I remain thoroughly ineffective,' I said.

'It looks a good book. Read me a meditation each morning after breakfast,' Douglas suggested, ignoring my grumbles.

I agreed to do so, inwardly praying that God would speak to me through the book. In my doubting state I wanted him to confirm what that kindly man had said at Waverley Abbey House.

When I began to use the book I found that it housed a family of minute insects. These little American bugs lived in the book's spine but some came out for a daily walk across the page as I read. They were beige-coloured, smaller that a pinhead. Some days four or five came out.

Other days I counted as many as twenty.

Those tiny creatures so fascinated me that one morning I looked at one through a magnifying glass.

'It's really cute. No wonder it can move so fast, it has six legs,' I told Douglas.

And at that moment God spoke to me, not in an audible voice, but deep within my heart: 'Those tiny insects that amuse you are part of my creation. Small as they are, they are important because I made them for a purpose. Each one has a function to fulfil. If tiny creatures like that have their place, why should you think I have no plans for you?'

I recalled some recently read words in Paul's letter to the Philippians: 'He who began a good work in you will carry it on to completion ...'.

I could not recall the rest of the verse, but that sufficed. God showed me that when I dubbed myself unproductive or worthless, I made him too small. Without intending to, I almost insulted him, belittling his ability to finish what he had begun in my life when I became his child.

This loving rebuke affected me profoundly. Affirmed! Uplifted! I still had a place in God's scheme of things and I thanked him for rebuking me in such a gentle and humorous way.

Shortly after this I received an airmail letter from the editor of *Decision* in Minneapolis. He told me of his plans for a new series of articles on 'the attributes of God' such as his love, faithfulness and loving-kindness, and invited me to write a two thousand word article for this series. Another writer would, he said, deal with the theological aspect. Mine should be a 'personal application article'.

I read the letter, then dropped it onto the breakfast table in dismay.

'Help!' I gasped. 'I've been asked to write an article about the God of Patience. How can I do that?'

'Why not? Haven't we been praying that you'll start writing again?' Douglas replied, helping himself to cereal.

Yes, we had prayed but I liked writing about topics on my own heart. Commissioned writing on someone else's chosen subject was a different matter.

'I've got to sign this contract form to say I'll do it,' I said.

'There's no need to decide now. Finish your breakfast,' Douglas advised.

That afternoon I pulled the letter out while we drank tea after Mrs Walton's Bible study.

'The *Decision* editor has asked me to write on the God of Patience but I can't do it,' I lamented.

Then, to my humiliation, I burst into tears.

'Listen, dear. Of course you can't do it in your own strength,' Mrs Walton said. 'But if God wants that article written, then he will enable you. Now just you do what King Hezekiah did when he received a disturbing letter.'

'Hezekiah?' I asked blankly.

'Yes, the letter that threatened invasion of his country. Instead of panicking, he spread that letter out before the Lord and begged him to intervene,' Mrs Walton reminded me. 'You go home and spread out your letter, then ask the

Lord if he wants you to write that article. Don't sign the contract today. If you sleep peacefully and awake with the assurance that God will enable you, then sign it and post it off tomorrow. If you still don't have peace, then wait a little longer.'

In Joan's absence, Morwen drove me home and I am glad she did.

'Honestly, Christine, I don't know why that letter's upset you,' she said. 'Knowing what I do of your past I can't see the problem. You've only to look back to see how patient God's been with you.'

Her words, crystal clear in their frankness, silenced my doubts. And she was right. The *Decision* editor had asked for a 'personal application' article but I had been too flustered to fully take it in. As Morwen turned into my road I saw the first glimmerings of possibility. Once home, I did exactly what Mrs Walton had advised. I knelt down and spread the letter out on the bed in front of me.

'Lord, I don't have to read this to you. You know what it asks me to do,' I prayed. 'Please, I need the help of your Holy Spirit to do it.'

That night I slept well, the deep, untroubled sleep of which Mrs Walton had spoken. Refreshed and confident of God's enabling, I signed the contract and airmailed it back to the States the next morning. And I thought about my past. What should I major in on, the good times or the bad?

While I pondered the possibilities I read a proverb written, I believe, by an Indian lady: 'The man who has no experience in the dark, has no secret to communicate in the light'. I appreciated that truth and it guided my thoughts, but I added two vitally important words to describe my own position: 'The man (or woman) who has no experience *of God* in the dark, has no secret to communicate in the light'. So, what had I discovered about the God of Patience in the dark places in my past?

I recalled a winter walk that I enjoyed when my knee had healed. I paused by a wooden gate to look at a field. A ploughman had gashed pleasant grassland into rows of bare furrows. Only a fleeing rabbit brought life to a scene that somehow filled me with sadness.

Months later I walked by that field again and gazed in delight. What a transformation! A carpet of golden corn shimmered in the sunlight. As I listened to the breeze whispering among the cornstalks, I thought: 'How patient God is! He knew the miracle of life, seed and growth that lay hidden in the soil. He was prepared to wait.'

God had been patient with me too. I thought of my teenage Christian days when I had such a thirst for Bible truth, and how I wanted it at once. I remembered that afternoon at a Girl Crusader camp when I slipped away to read my Bible alone in the woods. I had decided that God would reveal many wonderful truths from his Word that day. But God does not work to our timetable, so he revealed nothing. I did not know that we can't manipulate God like that. Nor did I realise what a patient God I had as I blundered on in my own time and way–heading for a spiritual backwater.

The Bible tells me that the Lord is 'the compassionate and gracious God, slow to anger, abounding in love and faithfulness ... forgiving wickedness, rebellion and sin'. As I continued my journey down memory lane I recalled how God sent Geoffrey to rescue me from the Exclusive Brethren, once I had repented of my stubborn waywardness. How he stood by me when Geoffrey died. How he led Douglas and me to one another. In all the years of our marriage that same infinitely patient God has gone on teaching me and never given up despite my slowness to learn.

After major surgery I had been advised to rest for several weeks but when a little strength returned I was impatient to be up and doing. Instead of tackling easy jobs, I decided to clear our loft of an accumulation of unwanted items.

'It's worse than an air raid the way things keep hurtling through the hatch,' Douglas complained.

Three days later pain and exhaustion forced me to stop. While waiting, low and dispirited, for physical renewal, I discovered that God had also been waiting to do a new thing in my life, not only physically but spiritually as well.

For several days I rested in my favourite chair beside the bedroom window. Once again dappled sunlight danced across the pages of my open Bible, as it had done in the woods so long ago. My eyes rested on the fruit of the Spirit listed in the fifth chapter of Galatians: love, joy, peace, patience ... Patience! I faced up to the fact that patience is a facet of God's character that he expects me to reflect.

The more I looked back, the more paragraphs for the *Decision* article formed in my mind. I thought again of that barren field, gouged with deep furrows. If the earth could sense pain, the turning of soil would be an uncomfortable experience, yet it produces a golden harvest.

This thought linked itself to some words in the Epistle of James: 'Be patient, then, brothers, until the Lord's coming. See how the farmer waits for the land to yield its valuable crop and how patient he is for the autumn and spring rains. You too, be patient and stand firm.'

As I saw again that field of waving corn in my mind's eye, I sensed that it would soon be time to put pen to paper. I had come to see that the God who works so patiently in nature can also work in my life if only I will yield it more fully to him, and 'keep in step with the Spirit'.

I picked up my pen to write that article, confident that the God of all patience would use the painful ploughings in my life to produce a harvest of love, joy, peace and, yes, even patience. Two thousand words flowed onto paper and I airmailed that article off to the States. I wasn't useless after all! God really did still have work for me to do. In the days ahead I found that it did not stop at article writing either.

Mrs Walton, who had been in ailing health for some time, asked me to lead the Bible studies for a few weeks. Over a cup of coffee I told her how much I had learned from the book of Daniel.

'Share what the Lord has been showing you,' Mrs Walton suggested.

I had never considered myself capable of running a Bible study, but I loved Daniel's story and the inspiration it gave me largely removed my apprehension. In my eagerness to share all that God had taught me, I had little time to be nervous.

Just before I began these studies, Douglas and I again went to Waverley Abbey House to spend a Partners' Week in the tranquillity of the lovely grounds and woodland. While there I also shared with Selwyn Hughes all that God had done in my life since my first visit.

'Trevor Partridge and I pray regularly for our partners,' Selwyn told me, 'and we prayed for you this morning. It's a privilege and joy for us to pray for your needs.'

I little imagined then that the following year I would be back at Waverley Abbey House to teach at a week-long Writers' Seminar. I had not taught at a Writing School since my *Decision* days but the old skills returned as if it had been only yesterday, and I thanked God for such enabling.

After Partners' Week, I shared such insights as I had on Daniel with Mrs Walton's Bible study group. I don't know how much they learned, but it greatly enriched my life leading those studies and I felt a pang of regret when we reached the last session. During those weeks I felt I had almost come to know Daniel as a personal friend–a friend with many valuable truths to share.

****

The winter after I taught at Waverley Abbey House I began to write this book. Creativity came slowly at first, then gradually words found their way onto paper more easily. During those early days it appeared a daunting task and I wondered if I would stay the course.

That Easter, Douglas and I went to Bournemouth for a week's rest and relaxation. Soon after our arrival at a favourite hotel, Morwen phoned me.

'Mrs Walton has been rushed into hospital with a stroke and other problems,' she told me. 'We're praying for her and I know you'll want to do so too.'

Dear, brave Mrs Walton. She had fought against illness and limitation for so long, yet her valiant spirit had never faltered. At eighty-one she made old age special– an example to the rest of us of how to grow old, not only gracefully, but in triumph.

On Easter Sunday she passed into the presence of the God she had loved for so long and served so faithfully. Psalm 92 says that 'the righteous will flourish like a palm tree ... they will still bear fruit in old age, they will stay fresh and green', and the psalmist's words described Mrs Walton precisely.

I returned from Bournemouth sad of heart, deeply aware of the loss of a valued friend and spiritual mother. Yet how could I not rejoice that her suffering had ended and that she would never shed another tear or know another twinge of pain?

The ladies of the Bible study group filled a whole row at the funeral service to pay grateful respect to the dear leader to whom we all owed so much.

That evening Peggy, a long-standing member of the

group, phoned me. 'While you were away we unanimously voted that you should be our new leader,' she said.

Later Joan added: 'You know, I'm sure Mrs Walton was training you for this when she asked you to lead those studies on Daniel.'

'If she was, I never suspected it,' I replied.

No panic. No dismay or cries of 'I can't'. My own calm amazed me. God had indeed been doing a new thing in my life. He had taught me, not only to go through hard experiences, but to GROW through them. The God of all patience had been training me for this task long before Mrs Walton did. So I accepted the position of leader, touched by the confidence that the other ladies placed in me.

'I feel a bit like Elisha must have felt when Elijah's mantle fell on him,' I confided to Joan. 'The one thing that bothers me is that I'm not like Mrs Walton. I don't have her charm or winsome ways.'

'We don't expect you to be a replica of Mrs Walton. We just want you to be yourself and do things your way. We know it will be different, but that's okay,' Joan assured me, and I appreciated her encouragement.

Yes, I floundered at first. Yes, I made mistakes. But no one criticized or condemned and I learned 'how' as I went along. I am still learning.

One day as I prepared for our study on Colossians I suddenly paused. Mrs Green used to run a ladies Bible study group! Had I really become *that much* like her? Amazing! Tears filled my eyes as they had done when, as a seventeen-year-old girl, I prayed: 'Please, Lord, make me like Mrs Green.' God had heard that prayer and began the lifelong process that prepared me for the answer. Had I known my prayer would involve a fifty-year training course, I may well not have dared to pray it.

Now, in the autumn of my life, I am not so concerned to be like Mrs Green, much as I treasure memories of her. Today I am more concerned with being Christlike. But then, when I look for human examples of Christlikeness, two loved faces will always stand out in my mental picture gallery, those of Mrs Green and Mrs Walton. With all my heart I thank God for the privilege of knowing two such stalwarts of the Christian faith.

And what about patience, that all-important fruit of the Spirit? The teaching of it has been a lesson to which God has returned again and again over the years. With slow learners like me it is not an 'instant' product but one that God carefully cultivates. Unlike me, he is not in a hurry.

And the future? I do not know what new tasks or problems will appear on my horizon as I travel on in my journey through Time. If allowed to choose, I would prefer to remain in safe and familiar waters rather than risk the turbulence of growth and change, but I need to remember that calm waters can also be stagnant. And so I rest in an inner assurance that, whatever comes my way, God will 'make it beautiful in its time'. And more, when my journey is over he will welcome me into the eternity in his presence upon which he has already set my heart.

****